THE FIRST
CHRISTMAS

THE FIRST CHRISTMAS

DENIS O'SHEA

Canon of the Holy Sepulchre

THE BRUCE PUBLISHING COMPANY

MILWAUKEE

NIHIL OBSTAT:

John A. Schulien, S.T.D.
Censor librorum

IMPRIMATUR:

✠ Moyses E. Kiley
Archiepiscopus Milwauchiensis

May 16, 1952

To

<small>His Excellency</small>

MOST REVEREND GERALD P. O'HARA, D.D.

ARCHBISHOP-BISHOP OF SAVANNAH-ATLANTA

APOSTOLIC NUNCIO TO IRELAND

Preface

IT IS a pity that so many good stories, recently written about the first Christians, are so lacking in verisimilitude. Their authors have not had the opportunity of seeing with their own eyes the scenes which they describe nor the advantage of a detailed knowledge of the period. There are, of course, many scholarly volumes dealing with the social, economic, religious, and political conditions of the first century, but they are too learned for the average reader. This book is an attempt to reconstruct the scenes of the first Christmas with all the authentic detail available and to present the events in the form of a story. Hence the style is narrative as far as possible, although some descriptions and explanations are inevitable. These, however, may add to the interest of the work, for most people would like to know the answer to such questions as: Who was the Caesar Augustus of the Christmas Gospel and why did he order a universal census? How was his decree brought from Rome and how was it published in Palestine? Was Herod as black as he is painted? What kind of house did Mary and Joseph have in Nazareth? How did they dress? What food did they eat? How much money could they raise for the trip? What vocal prayers did they say? What was their route from Nazareth to Bethlehem? What is the scenery like? Where did they put up at nights? What were the probable incidents of the long journey? Why were they refused admission to the inn? Was there really snow on the ground? Where was the stable? Are the ox and ass of the Crib authentic? What has become of the manger? What kind of people were the shepherds? In what form did the angels appear?

As the Scriptures themselves are the best commentaries on the Bible, the Books of the Old and New Testaments have been drawn upon to illustrate the manners and customs of the Holy Land.

His Holiness Pope Pius XII has been graciously pleased to bless and encourage the writing of this book.

Tang
County Westmeath
Ireland

Contents

THE FIRST
CHRISTMAS

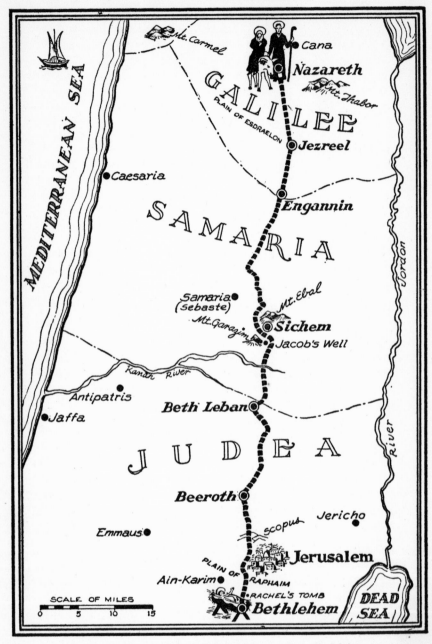

Route of Mary and Joseph from Nazareth to Bethlehem

CHAPTER 1

News for Nazareth

THE well of Nazareth is situated at the cross-roads at the north-eastern extremity of the town. Its source is a spring a few yards higher up the hillside to the west, from which the water flows down through an aqueduct. It is and always has been the sole source of spring water in the town. To this well the Blessed Virgin Mary, together with the other women of the town, directed her steps twice a day. Morning and evening she left her house in the town above and came down, pitcher on head, to the well by the cross-roads below. She took her turn with the other women and girls in lowering her pitcher into the cool dark depths of the well, and then returned up the narrow streets to her home. It was water from this well which quenched the thirst of Jesus, Mary, and Joseph for many years. The well is the only one of the sacred sites in Nazareth which has not been built over by the piety of generations, and cannot have changed much down the centuries. It remains today very much as it was in the days of the Holy Family, and so merits a description.

Probably the principal change is the metal piping. The open shaft down which the women of old lowered their vessels by ropes is now covered with stone. Instead, the water is drawn from three taps in a pipe above knee level. A stone arch still protects the women from the rays of the sun, and there is also a low stone wall which formerly prevented thirsty animals from falling into the open shaft. On this parapet the women still rest their pitchers while they lave their bare feet at the running taps within and enjoy a gossip. The donkey of the water-carrier must remain without while the water-skins are filled within.

Another change is that the picturesque pitcher is often replaced by the ugly but more serviceable gasoline cans which serve equally in carrying water, and the water-skins on the donkey by water-cans. As a rule men do not fetch water, but during the sweltering heat of the long dry summer the male water-carrier plys a profitable trade. He leads a donkey with skins full of the precious liquid, or carries two skins suspended from a stick across his shoulders, and wends his way through the streets of the town, selling cupfuls of cold water to those who wish to quench their thirst in the heat of the day. But the women of Nazareth still come to the well, with the graceful gait acquired by their habit of carrying pitchers or baskets on their heads. When filled under the tap, the pitcher is first elevated to the shoulder and then to the head, where a corner of the veil or a rolled cloth forms the pad upon which the weight is balanced. The raised right hand grasps the handle of the pitcher, which thus is tilted slightly to the right. Then with the left hand planted firmly on the hip as a counterpoise, the woman of Nazareth stalks up the hill to her home.

There has been a well at Nazareth from time immemorial. There is no reference to it in the Bible, but there is a beautiful description of the scene at a similar well at Nachor. Eliezer, Abraham's steward, came to Nachor to seek a wife for Isaac among the relatives of Abraham living there. "And when he had made the camels lie down without the town near a well of water in the evening, at the time when women are wont to come out to draw water" (Gen. 24:11). Every word of this text illustrates an Eastern custom. "He made the camels lie" — a mode of expression taken from actual life. The action is literally kneeling; not stooping, sitting, or lying down on the side like a horse, but kneeling on his knees, which the camel is taught to do from its youth.

The place is said to have been a well of water, and this well was outside the city. In the East, where wells are scarce and water indispensable, the existence of a well or fountain determines the site of the village. The people build near it, but prefer to have it outside the city, to avoid the noise, dust, and confusion always occurring near it, especially if it is situated on a public highway. It is around the fountain that the thirsty traveller and the wearied caravan assemble. If one is separated from one's company before arriving at a town, one need only inquire for the fountain, and there he will be reunited with his company. It was perfectly natural, therefore, for Eliezer to halt at the well. The time was evening; but it is further stated that it was when the women go forth to draw water. True to life again. At that hour the peasant returns home from his labour, and the women are busy preparing the evening meal, which is to be ready at sunset. Cold, fresh water is then in demand. As can readily be imagined, there is a great concourse around the well, where the news brought in by travellers is mingled with local gossip. But why limit the fetching of water to the women? Simply because such is the fact. "About great cities men often carry water, both on donkeys' and on their own backs; but in the country, among the unsophisticated natives, women only go to the well or the fountain; and often, when travelling, have I seen long files of them going and returning with their pitchers 'at that time when women go out to draw water.'"[1]

In the Gospel, Nazareth is described as "a city," that is, it was not an unfenced village but a walled town. After the conquest of the Promised Land, the people left behind them their nomadic habits and settled down to the cultivation of the soil.

Soon, however, the settlers found themselves molested by the wandering tribes from across the Jordan or from the deserts. These marauders would turn flocks loose in the standing corn of the tillers of the soil, and carry off the stored grain and cattle.

Sometimes they burned the homesteads, murdered the men, and took the women and children into slavery. So the husbandmen soon found, like the early settlers in America who were surrounded with Indians, that separate homesteads dotting the fields were a mistake. The necessity of protecting life and property from raiders compelled them to build their houses close together for mutual protection. This was the origin of the village, which grew into the city with the further protection of a wall around it. At night the fieldworkers retired to the safety of their walled town, like the sheep to the stone fold. Hence, the chief characteristic of a Palestinian city was its wall, which indeed gave it the right to be called a city (cf. Lev. 25:29). The site was usually determined by the proximity of a well or of a rocky height which could easily be defended.

The city wall had one or more gates which were closed and barred from sunset to sunrise. The primary purpose of the gate was to make secure the city, and the open space beyond the gateway was used for many social purposes. The women gossiped at the well, but the men assembled for graver discussion at the gate. Here, too, the tribunal of the magistrates was set up, and justice administered in summary fashion, so that the fieldworkers might not be delayed. The wide open space without the gate was the market place, where grain, wine, oil, cattle, vegetables, and the like were bought and sold. Here, too, public meetings were held, the money-changers set up their tables, labourers waited to be hired, and the children came out to play (cf. Matt. 11:16).

Within the walls each house had its inviolable privacy, for the door alone, not the windows, opened onto the street. The passersby outside could know nothing of what was taking place behind these blank walls, for the windows and balconies of the houses opened onto the inner courts. "He was as much outside as the dog at his feet. It is probable that the streets of Oriental towns have always by preference been narrow, sufficient for the foot-passenger and baggage animal, and affording shelter from the sun to the merchants and tradesmen. Such are the streets of Hebron and Zidon; and in Damascus the 'street called straight,' once a broad Roman carriage-way, with a foot-path on each side of the stately colonnade, now shows a return to the Oriental type."[2]

One winter's evening in Nazareth the files of women were coming and going as usual between the city gate and the well outside the wall. The clouds over the surrounding hills were lead-coloured, and the north wind from Mount Hermon was cold and raw. So the women wrapped their red, blue, or black veils more closely around them and quickened their steps. Nor did they loiter under the shelter of the vault to gossip for as long as was their wont on the long summer evenings.

Rebecca, at the well of Nachor, is described as "an exceeding comely maid, and a most beautiful virgin, and not known to man: and she went down to the spring, and filled her pitcher and was coming back" (Gen. 24:16). All Jewish women were descended from Rebecca, the wife of Isaac, the mother of Jacob, but there was a woman at the well of Nazareth who was more comely and chaste than even their venerated ancestress. The word Nazareth has been said to mean "flower" or, more correctly, "guardian."[3] Little did the women of Nazareth guess that Mary was the flower of the human race, "our tainted nature's solitary boast," and the mother-guardian of the Incarnate God. They knew her only as their neighbour, the young wife of Joseph the carpenter, and yet her presence amongst them has made Nazareth famous for all time. The cold of the weather did not repress the natural high spirits of the younger women and girls. They were laughing and chattering as they helped one another to raise the pitcher, so heavy when full, to the head. They laughed when the cold water splashed down on their faces, as they do to this day, and some of the younger ones fairly shrieked with merriment when they made a companion wince by squirting water into her face.

Suddenly one of the women uttered an exclamation and

pointed up the hill, over which the road from En-gannim wound down to the gateway. Instantly the chatter of tongues was hushed and the merriment ceased. The women kneeling by the shaft got up hastily, those advancing with empty pitchers stood still as statues, and those about to depart remained. All eyes were turned on the highway. What did they see? There were two men riding down the track on donkeys, one behind the other. There was nothing unusual in that. But behind the donkeys eleven soldiers marched in single file, and the fading light flashed on the line of helmets, shields, and spears. It was a decurion with his squad of ten.

Soldiers of the king were unusual visitors to this quiet town in the valley of the hills, and the women boded no good from their coming. At once they drew their veils modestly before their faces and retired under the stone vault of the well, where they huddled together like a flock of frightened sheep. The two elders rode past without a glance, for it was beneath their dignity to notice females. But the soldiers straightened their backs and stepped out more smartly, as is their wont under the gaze of women, heads erect under crested helmets, burnished shields swinging in time to the step, arms and armour jingling and rattling. They whistled, grimaced, and made ribald remarks to the women, as rude soldiers do, as they marched on with blaze of scarlet and glitter of steel until they halted at the gate. The two heavy wooden leaves of the gate, studded with iron nails, stood wide open, for it was not yet dark and the times were peaceful. As the gate-keeper hurried out, one of the elders called out to him authoritatively,

"Peace be to thee! We bear a message from Herod the King. Sound the shophar and summon the judges."

The watchman bowed obsequiously and hastened off. The two elders dismounted and stamped up and down to restore the circulation to their cold limbs. Behind them the decurion lined up his men facing the gateway. The women at the well were cut off from their homes by the soldiers, so they stayed where they were. In a few minutes they heard the deep, hoarse notes of the horn. Bells were not in use and the silver trumpets of the priests were reserved for the Temple and the battlefield. The shophar was made from the horn of a ram or wild goat, and was blown to announce the imminence of the Sabbath, for summoning to the synagogue, at excommunications, for proclamations, and the like.[4] As its raucous sound penetrated the narrow streets, the citizens broke off their business and hurried out to the market place, excited and alarmed by the unusual summons. The merchant left his booth, the artisan his bench, and even the peasants hurried in from their fields. Among the first to come were the magistrates, the seven men of substance to whom the preservation of law and order was entrusted. They, least of all, dare not linger, when the voice of Herod called. Soon they were exchanging salutations with the elders and casting apprehensive glances at the soldiers of the King.

The first of the two elders was one of the royal scribes. He was a chubby man, fattened by palace food, decked out with rings and chains, and wrapped in an immense mantle of the best camel's hair. His colleague was a priest from Jerusalem, a tall gaunt man with the thews and sinews of a butcher of the Temple. Though he was proud of his lineage as a son of Aaron, he was very respectful to the upstart scribe, from whom a word in the king's ear could accelerate or retard advancement. The soldiers were not Roman legionnaires who were stationed on the frontiers of Syria and were not under Herod's command. They were foreign mercenaries from one of the three regiments of Gauls, Thracians, and Germans employed by the King for the intimidation of his native subjects. At this time there were similar parties touring the provinces, bringing the King's message to every town from Dan to Beersheba. The smallness of the escort was indicative of the peacefulness of the province under the iron rule of the King. To the magistrates the scribe presented his credentials, a letter stamped with the royal seal. The ceremony was little more than a matter of form, for the presence of the military was proof enough that he came armed with the authority of the King. When the assembled people assumed an attitude of attention, a tense and boding silence prevailed and the scribe addressed them.

"Herod the King sends greetings to his good people of Nazareth."

The magistrates salaamed and the soldiers raised their spears in salute. There were a few subdued curses from the background, but these the scribe tactfully disregarded.

"Peace be to ye! An edict has gone forth from Caesar Augustus that the whole world shall be enrolled. As I, the King, am the friend of Caesar, I have decreed that this enrolling shall be made throughout my kingdom. Wherefore, let every man repair to the place of origin of his house and family and have his name inscribed in the public registers. I, the King, have spoken."

"Long live the King!" shouted the soldiers in his pay.

But there was no demonstration of loyalty from the multitude. Instead, the Nazarenes looked gloomily at one another, angry at this disturbance of their daily lives. This was the first census ordered by Rome in the Holy Land, and they resented it. Moreover, once their names were inscribed in the lists they might not so easily evade the payment of the poll-tax of a denarius. Their land, too, would be more accurately assessed for taxation. A muttering of discontent broke out, and imprecations even were uttered by the hardier patriots. "It is not lawful to pay tribute to Caesar! Why should we make journeys at the behest of the Edomite? Jehovah is the sole King of Israel!" But the magistrates trembled and were aghast when they heard the old war-cry of the Machabees raised in the rear. "Who is like unto Thee among the gods, Jehovah?"

It was clear that the Nazarenes regarded the edict as an offence to their religion, their patriotism, and their purses. But no man dared come forward and protest openly, for fear of the King lay like a shadow across the whole land. The scribe only smiled wearily and shrugged his shoulders, for he had heard similar murmurings in other towns of Galilee, and they had come to naught. He merely motioned to his colleague, the priest, to come forward and address the people, with the purpose of persuading them to resign themselves to the inevitable. This priest, unlike many others of the lower clergy, was a Herodian in politics, and he spoke as the mouth-piece of the High Priest Joazar.

"Men of Israel! Children of Abraham!" he began, and the people were soothed by the appeal to their race and religion. This Son of Aaron exerted all his eloquence to make an unpopular law popular. He pointed out that there was no novelty in numbering the people and that there was nothing against it on religious grounds, and he reminded them that both Moses and David had numbered the people. He quoted the texts: "And the Lord spoke to Moses in the desert of Sinai. . . . Take the sum of all the congregation of the children of Israel by their families and houses" (Num. 1:1–2). "And the king said to Joab the general of his army: Go through all the tribes of Israel from Dan to Bersabee, and number ye the people that I may know the number of them" (2 Kings 24:2). But the Nazarenes felt in their hearts that this census was different; that neither the pagan Caesar nor the usurper Herod could be compared with Moses, the divinely appointed Lawgiver, nor with David, the divinely appointed king. They felt that this census was the token of their servitude to heathen Rome and was incompatible with the theocratic character of Israel. This the political priest tried to explain away, using the name and authority of the high priest himself. He succeeded, not in convincing the Nazarenes, but in silencing their opposition. After all, the people had to obey, and well they knew it. But their motive for submitting was not the persuasion of the priest but the compulsion of the King. Behind the eleven soldiers lined up at the gate was the whole army of Herod, and behind Herod were the invincible legions of Rome.

Slowly, gloomily, in the fading light of the short winter

day, the good folk of Nazareth dispersed from the market place and returned through the gateway to their homes, to resume their interrupted occupations. Among them was Joseph the carpenter, whom the sound of the shophar had drawn from his bench and who had been an interested spectator. His neighbours respectfully saluted him as "Son of David," a title they would never dream of giving to the man who sat on the throne of David. Joseph was troubled, as was all of Nazareth. He had to bring home to Mary the news of the census and discuss with her, in the privacy of their home, the details of his departure. Her days were nearly accomplished that she should be delivered, and yet he saw himself compelled to leave her and journey across the mountains to Bethlehem, the place of origin of the house and family of David.

CHAPTER 2

The Census of Caesar

EVERY Christmas Day we stand up reverently in our churches
and listen again with wondering awe to the Gospel of the
Nativity. "In those days there went out a decree from Caesar
Augustus that the whole world should be enrolled." As children
we wondered about this man who could give orders to the
people of the whole world. We were told that he was the
emperor of Rome, the super-king of the world. His name and
titles were in the mouths of all men of the times, and the
shadow of his power loomed large over the earth. He knew
nothing of such poor folk as Mary and Joseph, dwelling far
away in provincial Palestine, and yet countless generations of
mankind since then have heard of Caesar Augustus only in
connection with the Babe of Bethlehem. "When Christ appeared
upon the earth, criminals ruled the world unopposed. He was
born subject to two sovereigns, the stronger far away at Rome,
the weaker and wickeder close at hand in Judea. One lucky ad-
venturer after wholesale slaughter had seized the empire, another had murdered his way to the throne of David and Solomon.
Each rose to high position through trickery, through civil wars,
betrayals, cruelty, massacres. They were born to understand one
another, were, as a matter of fact, friends and accomplices, as
far as was possible between a subordinate rascal and his rascal
chief."[1]

Who was this Caesar Augustus, whose decree was to cause such inconvenience to Mary and Joseph? His original name was Octavian; he was the son of a money-lender, but he was also the great-nephew and heir of the dictator Julius Caesar. In the year 44 B.C., Octavian, then a youth of nineteen, was studying rhetoric in Greece when he heard of the assassination of Caesar by the republicans. He hastened to Rome at once, to claim his great inheritance and to join with the political party which strove to avenge the memory of Caesar. It was proposed to march against Mark Antony who had seized power, but Octavian considered it wiser to make terms with this redoubtable soldier, especially as the millionaire Lepidus was disposed to take his side. Hence Antony, Lepidus, and Octavian formed a triumvirate to rule the Roman world. The first result of this alliance was the sacrifice of their relatives and best friends to each other's vengeance. For example, Octavian gave up Cicero to the vengeance of Antony, while Antony sacrificed his uncle and Lepidus his brother. Three hundred senators and two thousand knights also perished in this oblation to party hatred. Then the triumvirs marched against Brutus and Cassius, the republican leaders, whom they defeated at the battle of Philippi. Octavian pleaded illness and remained in his tent during the fighting. Though he took no personal part in the victory, he took the lion's share of the spoils, namely, the provinces of Italy, Gaul, and Spain. But his triumph did not slake his lust for revenge. He wished that the head of Brutus should be thrown at the foot of Caesar's statue; he had his principal prisoners strangled; he confiscated the lands of his political opponents and distributed them to his veterans. He managed to deprive Lepidus of the province which had fallen to his share, and opened hostilities against Antony who ruled in the East, with Alexandria as his capital. He declared that Antony had affronted his sister Octavia by refusing to take her back as his wife and preferring the foreign queen Cleopatra. Antony, the "mailed Bacchus," was defeated in the famous sea-fight off Actium in 31 B.C. He fled to Cleopatra in Egypt, but, as no hope remained, he stabbed himself, thus assuring the sole power to his ruthless rival.

Octavian had assumed the illustrious name of Caesar as part of his inheritance, and now his victorious legions hailed him as Imperator, Commander-in-chief. The most usual title for a sovereign was that of king, but the title was unpopular in Rome. Indeed the suspicion that Julius Caesar had been ambitious of a crown had been the cause of his death at the hands of the republicans. So Octavian was careful to avoid the insidious title and preferred to be known as Prince of the Senate. However, the obsequious senators hastened to confer upon their master the title Augustus, as one to whom religious veneration was due. More, they actually made a god of his late uncle. The decree of deification ran: "To the Genius of the divine Julius, father of his country, whom the Senate and the Roman People placed among the number of the gods." During his lifetime Augustus would not accept such worship of himself, at least by Roman citizens, though he was not so particular in the provinces and subject kingdoms. After his death, however, the Senate enrolled him, too, among the gods as the divine Augustus. In theory the Senate retained the government of the Roman people, but in reality all power was concentrated in the hands of Augustus, the chief executive. "To resume, in a few words, the system of the Imperial government, as it was instituted by Augustus and maintained by those princes who understood their own interest and that of the people, it may be defined as an absolute monarchy disguised by the forms of a commonwealth. The masters of the Roman world surrounded their thrones with darkness, concealed their irresistible strength, and humbly professed themselves the accountable ministers of the senate, whose supreme decrees they dictated and obeyed."[2]

The advent of Augustus to supreme power marked the end of the tremendous and protracted civil wars, and the Roman world entered upon an era of tranquillity. For the previous two hundred and five years the Temple of Janus had remained open, the sign that the State was engaged in strife the end of which no man could foresee, typified by the double faced head of the god, looking backward and forward. In time of war the Temple of Janus was left open, to indicate that the god had gone forth to assist the Roman arms; it was closed in time of peace, to ensure that the guardian god should not leave Rome. Augustus now had the honour of closing it; the third time in the whole history of Rome that it had been closed. He set himself the task of promoting the prosperity of the empire and of rebuilding the City. To use his own expression, he "found Rome built of brick and left it marble." His war-torn legions rested upon their arms in their camps upon the frontiers, in places so far apart as the chalk cliffs of northern Gaul and the edge of the Syrian desert, the cork-woods of Spain and the delta of the Danube. For once, even the foreign barbarian had sheathed the sword and refrained from raiding across the Roman border. Never had the peace seemed so complete and universal; the world seemed to repose under the wing of the Roman eagle, for the birth of the Prince of Peace was nigh.

> No war or battle's sound
> Was heard the world around;
> The idle spear and shield were high uphung;
> The hooked chariot stood,
> Unstained with hostile blood;
> The trumpet spake not to the armed throng;
> And kings sat still with aweful eye,
> As if they surely knew their sovran Lord was by.
> — MILTON

What was the master of the world doing before the birth of Christ? Augustus took advantage of the profound peace to reckon up the resources of the empire and to restore order to administration and finance, so disorganized by the civil wars. Like any merchant, the owner of the empire was taking stock, conning over his accounts, making out the inventory of his possessions; the *breviarium imperii*. Later on his successor Tiberius would produce this inventory. The historian Tacitus writes: "The senators turned to the statue of Augustus, and at times fell prostrate at the knees of Tiberius. Thus surrounded, he called for the state-paper, and ordered it to be read. It set forth an estimate of the empire and its resources, the number of citizens, the allies of Rome, the relation of naval strength, the names of the conquered kingdoms and provinces, the subsidies and tributes, and the amount of the revenue, with the necessary disbursements of government, and the demands for secret service. The whole was in the handwriting of Augustus."[3] For the compilation of this inventory Augustus decided to decree a universal census and have the names of all his subjects inscribed in the public registers. Taxation of land was the most profitable source of revenue, and the vast survey initiated by Julius Caesar was now completed. All subjects between the ages of fourteen and sixty were liable to a poll-tax of one denarius. When their names were enrolled and their property assessed, the work of the publicani or tax-collectors would be facilitated, and an immense regular income would flow into the coffers of the state. Once the census was completed in each province and kingdom, no one could easily evade payment. Augustus decided, and his will was law. Out from Rome on the great wide roads north and south galloped the couriers with copies of the imperial edict in their saddlebags. Out from the port sped the swift galleys to carry the edict of Augustus across the seas. "And it came to pass that in those days there went out a decree from Caesar Augustus; that the whole world should be enrolled."

"The whole world!" A grandiose phrase of the evangelist! But St. Luke was a subject of Caesar, for him almost the whole known world was comprised within the empire. All the lands washed by the waters of the Mediterranean, in Europe, Asia, and Africa were included in the empire, for the Mediterranean had become a Roman lake. The grandeur of Rome, the glory of Greece and the isles, Asia Minor and Syria, Egypt and proconsular Africa, Mauretania, Spain, Gaul, Germany west of the

Rhine, the Balkan lands south of the Danube, all were united in the mightiest state the world had ever seen. The many diverse races retained much of their own culture, customs, and religion, but Roman law, Roman governors, and Roman legions united them all. The city on the Tiber had become the capital of the world. "A city greater than any upon earth, whose amplitude no eye can measure, whose beauty no imagination can picture, who raises a golden head amid the neighbouring stars and with her seven hills imitates the seven regions of heaven, mother of arms and of law, who extends her sway over all the earth and was the earliest cradle of justice, this is the city which, sprung from humble beginnings, has stretched to either pole, and from one small place extended its power so that upon it the sun never sets."[4]

Beyond the boundaries not much of the world was known. To the east there was Parthia, an undefined area, of which St. Luke would know something, for as recently as 53 B.C. the Parthians had defeated a Roman army under Crassus and restored for a while a Hasmonean prince to the throne of Jerusalem. There, too, was Persia, whose "Great King" was the enemy of the Greeks, but had been laid low by Alexander the Great, who had led his invincible phalanxes across the Persian hills to the confines of mysterious India, then regarded as the limit of the habitable earth, as his weary veterans had complained: *Paene in ultimo mundi fine consistimus*[5] (We stand nearby at the farthest boundary of the earth). To the west, beyond the Pillars of Hercules, now known as the Straits of Gibraltar, there rolled the waters of a vast and uncharted ocean. To the north beyond the cliffs of Gaul was the ultima Thule of the earth. A literary man, as St. Luke was, would have read the Commentaries of Julius Caesar, in which that great man described how he had invaded Britain in 55 B.C. His uncle's book was, of course, familiar to Augustus from his youth.

In the subject kingdoms which still enjoyed comparative independence an imperial census had been aimed to include only adult males of military age. But this census of Augustus was framed in accordance with the old law of Rome, and so the names of old men, women, and children were required for registration. The reasons for this extension may be found in the relations which existed between the emperor and his friend King Herod. Now Herod, though he ruled Judea, was not by birth a Jew. The absence of his pedigree from the genealogical records piqued him, and so in a fit of despotic anger he attempted to burn the public archives.[6] Was this extension of the census meant to annoy Herod and give him the trouble of having the registers reconstituted? It would be like Augustus to play such a sly trick on his friend. Whether this explanation be true or not, it is too much in accordance with the character of Augustus not to be indicated.[7]

CHAPTER 3

The House of Herod

PALESTINE is a small country; so small that St. Jerome was apologetic about its area when writing to Dardanus, the prefect of the large and important province of Gaul: "We are ashamed to speak of the extent of the Promised Land, lest we appear to have given to the pagans an opportunity for mockery."[1] Palestine, even at its greatest extent under Solomon, could not rival the area of its neighbours, the mighty monarchies of Assyria and Egypt. Nor was the size of the state always the same, for it fluctuated with the fortunes of its rulers. For example, the kingdom had sunk to the size of a county before its conquest by the Babylonians. Herod's kingdom contained about ten thousand square miles of territory. It was thus only about a third of Ireland (approximately the size of the state of Maryland). This pocket-kingdom was tucked away in a corner of the great imperial province of Syria, of which it formed a part. But "the weak things of the world hath God chosen, that he may confound the strong" (1 Cor. 1:27), and the littleness of Israel bore no proportion to its importance as the theatre of the greatest events in the history of the world. For here, to quote Shakespeare, are

> *Those holy fields*
> *Over whose acres walked those blessed feet*
> *Which fourteen hundred years ago were nailed*
> *For our advantage to the bitter cross.*

This little land is bounded on the west by the Mediterranean Sea, on the east by the Jordan Valley, shut in by the mountain range of Lebanon on the north, and bordered by the rocky desert on the south. Along the coast there is a narrow plain, then the land rises in a chain of hills, beyond which it sinks into the deep fissure of the Jordan. The country is so small that the snow-clad Mount Hermon in the extreme north is sometimes visible from the shores of the Dead Sea in the south. From several of the central hills one can see the opposite limits of the land, the silver sheet of Lake Genesareth and the purple mountains of Moab to the east, and the green ridge of Carmel rising over the sea in the west. Besides, the brilliant sunshine, the bright skies, and the crystalline transparency of the atmosphere make far-off outlines distinctly visible, giving the impression that distant objects are close at hand.

What was the population of the Holy Land in the first century of the Christian era? The only contemporary figures available are found in the works of Flavius Josephus. He states that in the province of Galilee alone there were no less than 240 towns, and he speaks almost indifferently of these as "villages" or "cities."[2] He adds: "The towns too are thickly distributed, and even the villages, thanks to the fertility of the soil, are all so densely populated that the smallest of these contains above fifteen thousand inhabitants."[3] On these figures the towns and villages of Galilee contained 3,600,000 people, and there were two other provinces, namely Samaria and Judea, besides outlying territory. Josephus is suspected of exaggeration, of writing to enhance the importance of his country in the minds of his Greek and Roman readers, but there is no other source extant against which his figures can be checked. He tells us, too, how the number of people present at a Passover in Jerusalem was calculated. He relates how the priests counted the number of lambs that were sacrificed and that the total came to 256,000 victims. He adds that a group of not less than ten persons partook of each lamb, so this would mean that not less than 2,565,000 people celebrated the Passover in that particular year in the reign of Nero.⁴ Among these there must have been a large proportion of foreign Jews from outside the country, but nevertheless the total is very great. In another place he relates that when Cestius Gallus, the governor-general of Syria, "was come to Jerusalem upon the approach of the feast of Unleavened Bread, the people came to him not fewer in number than three million"⁵ to complain about his subordinate in Judea. If the figures of Josephus be admitted, and he was a contemporary, the population of the Palestine of his day must have been approximately eight million souls.⁶

The Gospels give the impression of a crowded land. Again and again we read of "multitudes" and of "great multitudes." The reign of Herod was the peak period of Palestine's prosperity. He gave his country thirty years of peace. Business boomed as never before, so much so that the King, without reducing his subjects to poverty, was able to extract vast sums not only to send as tribute to Caesar, but also to carry out his grandiose building schemes. The country was then far more flourishing than it is today, with 700,000 refugees deprived of house and land, and with Arab and Jew glowering at each other across an artificial frontier in the city of Jerusalem itself. In the first century the cities were larger and full of new and imposing buildings. The ports of Caesarea and Ptolemais were crowded with sails and were rapidly expanding. In the provinces the villages and towns must have been on a larger scale. The hillsides were cultivated on the terrace system, only traces of which now remain. "The fertile plains along the coast or interspersed among the hills of Samaria and Galilee were more completely cultivated. The irrigation, which is still in some parts very good, was more widely extended. Though the west of the Jordan was never thickly timbered, there were probably many more trees growing in the open, and especially many more fruit trees than there are at present. The discontent that existed then as it exists now, was due to moral causes and not to material pressure. The

General view of Nazareth

— PROF. C. C. MC COWN; FROM "LADDER OF PROGRESS,"
BY PERMISSION HARPER AND BROS.

Hill of Samaria from the north

— AMERICAN SCHOOLS OF ORIENTAL RESEARCH

Semicircular Israelite tower, Samaria

aspect of the land must indeed have been bright and smiling; and if there were volcanic fires beneath the surface, they were not the product of despair, but rather of irrepressible hope and energy."[7]

At the end of September, 1942, the British official figure for the census of all Palestine was 1,613,376, of whom 478,500 were Jews. Since then the British have withdrawn. The new Israeli government now controls about half the country from which the Arabs were dispossessed. At the census of November 8, 1948, the population of the Israeli territory was 713,000 Jews, with 69,000 Christians and Arabs. There are no recent figures available for the half of Palestine which still remains under the Arabs. There has been a large volume of Jewish immigration since the census of 1942, so that the two million mark for all Palestine has now probably been passed. Even so, on the estimate based on the figures of Josephus, the population of Palestine in the first century was four times greater than it is at present.

Who was Herod, the man who reigned as king of the Jews when our Lord was born? He was neither Jew, Greek, nor Roman. His father, Antipater, was an Edomite or Idumean, one of a people forcibly converted and circumcised by a Jewish conqueror in the preceding century. His mother, Cypros, was an Arab lady, so Herod had not a drop of Jewish blood in his veins. The name conferred by Antipater on his son shows how little he was influenced by the true religion, for "Herod" means "hero-born," and is derived from pagan mythology. How did such a foreign upstart come to sit upon the throne of David and Solomon? Antipater laid the foundations of the fortunes of the family, and his son inherited his shrewd policy of supporting Roman power in the east. But Herod himself was really great, great in ability and ambition, great in war and great in peace. Josephus gives us the above parentage of Herod which, though foreign, was respectable.[8] But the ancestry of Antipater has been preserved elsewhere, and in the eyes of the Jews it was abominable. The historian Eusebius, relying upon the earlier Julius

Africanus, relates that Antipater was the son of a slave attached to a pagan temple in Ascalon. "Herod, the first foreigner, was given the kingdom of the Jews by the Romans. As Josephus relates, he was an Idumean on his father's side and an Arabian on his mother's. But Africanus, who also was no common writer, says that they who were more accurately informed about him report that he was a son of Antipater, that the latter was the son of a certain Herod of Ascalon, one of the so-called temple-slaves of the temple of Apollo. This Antipater, having been taken prisoner while a boy by Idumean robbers, lived with them, because his father, being a poor man, was not able to pay a ransom for him. Growing up in their practices, he was afterwards befriended by Hyrcanus, the High Priest of the Jews."[9] No wonder that the Jews, so proud of their own ancestry as the Chosen People of God, hated their foreign King of servile and idolatrous origin.

Antipater had been appointed governor of Idumea by Alexander Jannaeus, king and high priest of the Jews. On Alexander's death his widow, Alexandra, with the help of the Pharisees, seized power. Her elder son Hyrcanus she allowed to officiate as high priest, but her younger son Aristobulus wanted to reign, and on her death civil war broke out between the brothers. Antipater took the part of Hyrcanus, the legitimate king. During the struggle an event occurred which revolutionised the politics of the East. In 64 B.C. the Roman general Pompey deposed the last Seleucid king and made Syria a Roman province. Antipater had the political acumen to realise that this meant the end of independence for the petty kingdoms of the East. He could no longer hope to rule an autonomous Palestine as the vizier of the easy-going Hyrcanus. Thereupon he adopted the policy of supporting the Romans at all costs, of becoming their most humble and obedient servant, and thereby to win their favour and protection for himself and his patron Hyrcanus. So he set to work diplomatically to gain Pompey's recognition of Hyrcanus as king of the Jews. Aristobulus, on the contrary, was foolish enough to fight, so Pompey conquered the country and took him prisoner. Hyrcanus was recognized as high priest and ruler, but was forbidden to use the title of king.

In 54 B.C. Crassus became proconsul, and needed money for the war against the Parthians. Antipater had the onerous task of handing over the Temple treasure to the Roman, and he did it. Although Crassus was defeated and slain, Antipater never wavered in his loyalty to Rome. When the great civil wars began, he must have been sorely puzzled as to which party was the Roman government. He continued to support Pompey, but when Pompey fell in 48 B.C. he rushed to the rescue of the victor, Julius Caesar. By him he was made a Roman citizen and governor of Judea under Hyrcanus. His son Herod, now 25 years old, obtained the governorship of Galilee, where his success in suppressing the Galilean irregulars won him the favour of the Romans and the suspicion of the Jews. When Caesar was stabbed by the republicans at the foot of Pompey's statue in 44 B.C., Antipater and Herod became zealous republicans. Then Antipater was poisoned by a rival whom he had generously saved from execution by the republicans, and in 43 B.C. Herod succeeded to the power and the policy of his father.

The historian Josephus extols Antipater as "a man distinguished for piety, justice, and patriotism."[10] Josephus, however, was a partisan of the House of Herod. Other authors maintain that Antipater had one notable virtue which Josephus overlooked entirely. Considering him as a product of the times, Antipater was "a remarkably merciful man; nor massacres or assassinations or even judicial murders are recorded of him. It is ironic that this amiable trait should have proved fatal to him. His son was to learn by his father's experience."[11]

At the intercession of Herod, Cassius, one of Caesar's assassins who now commanded in Syria, had the enemy of Antipater killed. Herod notably strengthened his position by his marriage with Mariamne, the granddaughter of Hyrcanus. He thus became a member of the royal house and, should old

Hyrcanus die, he would be the natural regent for the heir, Mariamne's brother, the younger Aristobulus, who was then ten years old. But Herod's patrons, the republicans Brutus and Cassius, were defeated at Philippi in 42 B.C., and Octavian and Mark Antony became the rulers of the Roman world. The East fell to Antony and Herod transferred his allegiance to him. At this time his fortunes were at their lowest ebb. The Parthians invaded Palestine and put the Hasmonean prince Antigonus on the throne, so Herod was compelled to flee to Rome. There he had little difficulty in persuading Antony and Octavian that he would make a more loyal vassal than the pro-Parthian Antigonus, so they had him proclaimed king by the Senate in 40 B.C. Herod thus succeeded beyond his wildest expectations, for the legitimate line of the Hasmonean priest-kings was set aside in his favour, and he became king in his own right, if not by the grace of God, then by the favour of the Roman senators. Preceded by the consuls and great magistrates of Rome, walking between Antony and Octavian, Herod was solemnly escorted up to the capitol, where sacrifice on his behalf was solemnly offered to the gods! That night Antony gave a banquet to celebrate the first day of the reign of Herod.

Herod was now king of the Jews, but he had yet to conquer his kingdom. The Roman legions, however, soon cleared out the Parthians, and the legitimate king, Antigonus, was beheaded. Herod had to wade through the blood of his Jewish subjects to ascend the throne, ruining the Hasmoneans, the benefactors of his father and himself. He managed to keep the patronage of Antony, despite the enmity of Cleopatra, who wanted Judea for herself. Civil war again broke out, this time between Antony and Octavian. Herod supported Antony and sent him money and supplies. Fortunately for him he was prevented from taking a personal part in the campaign against Octavian, for Cleopatra had sent him off to subdue the Nabatean Arabs. He was successful in this, but when he returned he heard the staggering news that Antony had been defeated at the famous sea-fight off Actium in 31 B.C. Before setting off to justify himself to Octavian, he eliminated any possible rivals at home. The young Aristobulus already had been "accidentally" drowned in the swimming pool of Jericho, and now old Hyrcanus, the benefactor of his father, was executed. Hence there was no male left of the House of Hasmon for Octavian to put on the throne. Nevertheless, Herod's position as a client of Antony was hazardous. He knew that he might lose both his head and his kingdom and that he faced the greatest crisis of his life. He decided on the bold course of visiting the conqueror, now resting on his laurels at Rhodes. But before he set sail, he gave secret orders that if he did not return his beautiful wife Mariamne should be slain, for he could not bear to think of her being given to another man.

Herod obtained an audience with Octavian, now the undisputed master of the Roman world. Before he entered the presence chamber, Herod humbly took the crown from his head. Would he ever put it on again? Would his head be left on his shoulders? Standing crown in hand before Octavian, he followed a bold but judicious line. Instead of apologising for his support of Antony, he stressed it, and declared that in the future he would be just as loyal to Octavian, if he were accepted as the friend and ally of the Roman people. Octavian knew that Herod was an able and useful client-king, and that he could help to pacify his section of the troublesome Eastern frontier. He knew, too, that Herod's speech was perfectly sincere and that his record proved that he was anxious to support the ruling power in the empire. So Octavian graciously bade him put on his crown and confirmed him in his kingdom. More, he actually augmented Herod's dominions and ever afterwards trusted him as a loyal friend.[12] Thus Herod, to the chagrin of his enemies, the bulk of both his Jewish and Gentile subjects, returned triumphantly to his capitol, more powerful than ever. At this time he was about thirty-five years of age, and there were still thirty-five years of life before him. His political vicissitudes were over, for Augustus was his patron for the rest of his life. Although he had been found so often on the losing side in the Roman civil wars, Herod's diplomacy each time enabled him to conciliate the conqueror and consolidate his position.

CHAPTER 4

Politics in Palestine

WHAT was the religion of Herod the Great? Due to political expediency he professed Judaism, the religion of the bulk of his subjects, for otherwise he might have been deposed by Augustus and replaced by a ruler more acceptable to the troublesome Jews. Herod nevertheless tolerated the religion of his other subjects; for example, the Samaritans, the Arabs, and the many worshippers of the Greek gods of Olympus. He built temples to Rome and Augustus at Caesarea, Sebaste, and Panium to conciliate his pagan subjects and demonstrate his loyalty to his over-lord. No wonder, then, that the people suspected that he went up to worship in the Temple of Jerusalem with the same motive with which he had ascended the capitol in Rome. However, he went out of his way to soothe the susceptibilities of the Pharisees. In arranging matches for the members of his family he refrained from breaking the prohibition against mixed marriages. Syllaeus, the vizier of the Nabatean Arabs, asked for the hand of his sister Salome, but as the Arab refused to accept circumcision and the Jewish faith Herod rejected his proposal, although it would have secured the alliance of a powerful neighbour. He respected the Mosaic prohibition of graven images and his coinage displayed neither his own head nor Caesar's nor the image of any living thing. In Jerusalem he erected a new palace, theatre, and hippodrome in the classical style, but they were devoid of any statues or sculptures which would offend the Pharisees. Not until the end of his days, when they conspired against him in favour of his brother Pheroras, did he cease to conciliate the Pharisees and break the commandment against graven images.

The political status of Palestine was that of a vassal kingdom within the Roman Empire. Herod's official title was *Rex Socius,* allied king, and his power was limited only by his allegiance to his over-lord. Within his kingdom the lives and fortunes of his subjects were in his hands. Provided he kept the peace with his neighbouring states, did nothing to jeopardise Roman interests, and paid tribute to Caesar, he could rule as he pleased. He maintained a standing army of foreign mercenaries and a host of secret police. Hence there were no rebellions during his reign and the few conspiracies against him were detected at once. Organised brigandage, formerly the curse of the kingdom, he ruthlessly repressed. If he were an oppressor, he had the merit of being the only one, for be brooked no other, and he protected his subjects from rapine. The Sanhedrin had been the supreme council of state, but it had opposed Herod's rise to power, and so he deprived it of much of its authority. The old hereditary nobility had espoused the cause of the legitimate dynasty, so Herod executed many of its members and confiscated their estates. He established a privy council on the Hellenic model, to which he appointed some of his relatives and his principal ministers. This new council of state was also the supreme court of justice, before which Herod had even members of the royal family arraigned. His councillors had for the most part Greek names, but this does not necessarily imply that they were pagans. Greek names were popular with all classes, as in the cases of Alexander, the high priest's kinsman (cf. Acts 4:6), Philip the Apostle, and Stephen the deacon. However, Nicolas of Damascus, the court historian and the king's mentor in philosophy as well as his ambassador to Rome, was certainly a pagan. So was Diophantus, the secretary of state, for no true believer would bear a name that smacked of blasphemy. One Ptolemy was grand vizier towards the end of the reign, and he may have been a Jew, but the other Ptolemy was certainly a pagan, for he was the brother of Nicolas. These were Herod's principal ministers.

In the past the high priest had been the head of the theocratic state of Israel and had held office for life. The Machabees were members of the priestly House of Hasmon, and by their successful wars for faith and fatherland had been awarded the crown by the grateful people. So for the past hundred years each Hasmonean king had been high priest as well. But family feuds had separated the offices. Hyrcanus became high priest on the death of his father, King Alexander Jannaeus, but his younger brother Aristobulus wanted to be king. Upon his accession, Herod reinstated old Hyrcanus as high priest, but afterwards had him executed as a possible rival for the throne, before he sailed to Rhodes for his fateful audience with Augustus. There remained the younger Aristobulus, the brother of Mariamne, the sole surviving male of the House of Hasmon, and as such the legitimate high priest. When this youth of sixteen had pontificated in the Temple, he had received such an ovation from the people that Herod in jealous fear had him drowned.

Who, then, was to be high priest? The King could not officiate, for he was not descended from Aaron and, hence, was not a priest. But he could appoint one of the lower clergy, a priest so humble that he could have no pretensions to rival the King. Herod, therefore, abolished the hereditary pontificate and broke the principle of office for life by nominating and deposing high priests at his pleasure. His first nominee was one Ananel, an obscure priest from Babylon. His next was Jesus the son of Phabet, of whom nothing was known. The third was Simon Boethos from Alexandria, who held office for seventeen years. The next was Matthias the son of Theophilus, who was deposed after a year, apparently for not preventing the removal of the golden eagle from the Temple. The last high priest to be appointed by Herod, and who survived him, was Joazar, the son of the above Simon Boethos. Apart from nominating and deposing the high priests, Herod does not seem to have interfered in the spiritual affairs of the Jews. For example, though he had rebuilt the Temple at enormous cost, he remembered that he was a layman and did not trespass on the sanctity of the inner courts reserved for the priests.

Joazar was high priest when our Saviour was born. Indeed, four sons of Simon Boethos were to attain the same dignity. They do not seem to have belonged to any of the families of the chief priests of the twenty-four courses into which the whole priesthood was divided. In fact, they were foreign Jews, natives of Alexandria. How, then, had they attained such eminence in Israel? The rise of the House of Boethos was due to one of its women. Josephus tells the story: "There was one Simon, a citizen of Jerusalem, the son of Boethos, a citizen of Alexandria, and a priest of note there; this man had a daughter, who was esteemed the most beautiful woman of that time; and when the people of Jerusalem began to speak much in her commendation, it happened that Herod was much affected by what was said of her: and when he saw the damsel, he was smitten with her charms. Yet did he entirely reject the thoughts of using his authority to abuse her, as believing what was the truth, that by so doing he would be stigmatised for violence and tyranny, so he thought it best to take the damsel to wife. And while Simon was of a dignity too inferior to be allied to him, but still too considerable to be despised, he governed his inclinations after the most prudent manner, by augmenting the dignity of the family, and making them more honourable. So he immediately deprived Jesus the son of Phabet of the high priesthood, and conferred the dignity upon Simon, and thus joined in affinity with him by marrying his daughter."[1]

Herod's first wife had been Doris, an Idumean like himself, but he divorced her to marry the beautiful Hasmonean princess Mariamne. In 29 B.C. he had Mariamne executed in a fit of jealousy and so was free to marry Simon's daughter who was also named Mariamne. This third wife became the mother of another Herod who married Herodias. They were the parents of Salome the dancer. Thus Joazar was related to the King, but was no longer his brother-in-law, for Mariamne had been divorced for complicity in a plot. Unlike most of the higher clergy, Joazar was a Pharisee, not a Sadducee, and thus had considerable influence with the people. We know for a fact that ten years later Joazar used this influence to persuade the people to submit to another Roman census.[2] Hence it is very probable that he was willing to assist Herod in this census of Augustus.

Herod is known to posterity as the Great, and he was great, great in his ability, his diplomacy, and his building. But his strangest claim to greatness lies in the fact that, once firmly established on the throne, he gave his country over thirty years of peace and prosperity, a halcyon period preceded by eras of war and devastation and to be followed after his death by the fatal rebellion against Rome and the extinction of the Jewish state. Such was the King who reigned before the coming of Christ. He was the "hero-born," the brutal despot, the brilliant diplomatist, the benefactor of his people, who was hated by his Jewish subjects because he was not born a Jew and by his pagan subjects because he professed to be a Jew. He was now a bloated old man of seventy, afflicted by a shameful disease and nearing the end of his days.

When the imperial courier dismounted outside the magnificent new palace in Jerusalem, he was hurried through the gates and given audience at once, for he brought a letter from Augustus, the master of the Roman world. He found the aged King reclining on a divan, for his body was racked by the pain of his incurable disease. On his knees the courier presented the rescript. As etiquette prescribed, Herod rose to his feet, bared his head, pressed the letter to his breast and kissed it. He dared not omit these marks of respect, for the courier would be sure to report how the rescript was received. Then Herod handed the letter to his secretary Diophantus to examine if the wrappings were unbroken and the seal intact, no unnecessary precautions in those days. The courier of Caesar was thanked and civilly dismissed with such presents as befitted his rank and importance. As Diophantus read aloud the terse Latin of the official document, Herod on his divan must have groaned with annoyance, for the order to hold a census created a thorny problem. Instantly the council of state was summoned, including Ptolemy the grand vizier, Nicolas the foreign secretary, and Joazar the high priest.

The edict of Augustus must be obeyed — King and councillors were agreed to that. But how would the people respond to such an innovation as a census? The pagan subjects might make no difficulties, but they were in the minority. The vast bulk of the people were Jews who resented bearing the yoke of Rome and would be sure to kick against this fresh application of the goad. The councillors remembered that when Augustus, about twenty years previously, had decreed a census in Gaul, the Gauls had bitterly opposed it as an unprecedented innovation. They had actually broken out in rebellion, and the census had to be postponed until the rebellion was suppressed. Herod was quite capable of dealing with a rebellion of his subjects, especially since he would have the support of the Roman legions in Syria, but he preferred to use peaceful means to persuade his people to submit. After the extirpation of a rebellion by fire and sword there would be less people to enrol and less property to assess.

Herod's solution of the problem was characteristic of his diplomacy. He would hold the Roman census in his kingdom but not by the Roman method. It was the Roman custom to enrol people in their actual place of residence. The Jews would resent this method, so he would number the people according to their own customs. From ancient times the Jews had been organised into twelve tribes, subdivided into families and then into households. If any man had moved from the place of origin of his

house and family, he would be sure to bring back or send back
the names of any children born to him abroad, thus keeping his
genealogy up to date. Josephus testifies to the fact that these
lists were carefully preserved and that the "public records" were
to be found at the headquarters of the tribe.[3] Ezra mentions
that some members of the House of Aaron were not allowed to
officiate as priests because their names were not found in the
official genealogies: "And could not shew the house of their
fathers, nor their seed, whether they were of Israel. . . . These
sought their writing in the record, and found it not: and they
were cast out of the priesthood" (2 Esd. 7:61, 64).

Thus King and council decided to carry out the census
of Caesar according to the clan system of the people. Every man
who resided at a distance from the place of origin of his house
and family would be allowed to return there to be enrolled.
This was a less convenient method, but it had the merit of being
in accord with the national feeling and less likely to provoke re-
sistance. Besides, it was good Roman policy to respect national
customs as far as possible. Herod, therefore, dictated the order
and Diophantus the secretary wrote it down. There and then the
scribes in the palace were set to work making many copies for
transmission to the towns. The high priest Joazar set about the
selection of suitable priests to persuade the people to submit.
Soon the officials were hastening out through the gates of
Jerusalem to proclaim the enrolling in every town and village of
that populous, prosperous land. And after not many days the
decree of Caesar was proclaimed in a city of Galilee called
Nazareth.

CHAPTER 5

Mary and Joseph Obey

NIGHT was falling when Joseph returned home from the meeting in the market place. It was too dark to work any longer and perhaps just time enough to close up the shop for the night. The carpenter's shop of Joseph's day was not too much unlike the modern shops in Nazareth today: open to the street without either door or window, but fixed so as to be closed at night by shutters. At night Joseph's workshop became the stable of his donkey, the sturdy beast used in transporting logs of wood too heavy for his own back. In lands of the East where there are no metalled or concrete roads the ass is most useful, for it is surefooted in steep or miry places where the flat-hooved horse would slip or founder. I have often seen heavily laden asses going up and down flights of steps in the old quarters of Jerusalem. Joseph would not turn his valuable beast of burden loose in the streets at night or leave it in a field beyond the walls lest it be stolen. At dusk large flocks of sheep or herds of goats were, of course, not brought into the town, but were confined in stone pens out in the fields where, owing to the danger from thieves and wolves, they were watched all night by shepherds or goatherds. But each man brought home his donkey or cow or milch goat at night, and it was the natural thing to stable his beast on his own premises. Since many of the dwellings consisted of two rooms only, the beast was accommodated in the outer, while the family ate and slept in the inner room.

Doctor Thomson has described the home-coming of oxen and asses to the safety of a walled town, not indeed Nazareth, but nearby Tiberias. "How sweetly the day draws to a close around this warm and delightful lake! and there come the droves of cattle and donkeys down from the green hills where they pasture! I have seen no place where there are so many, or at least where they are brought home together, and in such crowds. Last night the thought struck me as they were entering the gate, and away I hurried after them, to see whether these Tiberian donkeys were as wise as those Isaias mentions. True to life, no sooner had we got within the walls, than the drove began to disperse. Every ox knew perfectly well his owner, his house, and the way to it; nor did he get bewildered for a moment in the mazes of these narrow and crooked alleys. As for the asses, they walked straight to the door, and up to their master's 'crib,' without turning to bid good-night to their companions of the field. I followed one company clear into their habitation, and saw each take his appropriate manger, and begin his evening meal of dry tibn. Isaias says in all this they were wiser than their owners, who neither knew nor considered, but forsook the Lord, and provoked the Holy One of Israel. These 'cribs' of Isaias are, I suppose, the 'mangers' of the New Testament, in one of which the infant Redeemer was laid."[1] "The ox knoweth his owner, and the ass his master's crib: but Israel hath not known me, and my people hath not understood" (Isa. 1:3).

In the fading light Joseph made up his dumb servant's bed from the bales of straw piled in the workshop, and filled the crib with its meal of tibn. This provender was not oats, but chopped straw mixed with herbs or salt to make it palatable. He then tidied up his workshop, put away his tools in their racks, and barred up the entrance to make all secure for the night. Then he entered the inner room to discuss with Mary the edict of Caesar and its bearing on their lives.

Mary, meanwhile, had lighted the lamp and put fresh fuel

on the fire, so that the room was bright and warm when Joseph came in from the cold, dark workshop. Firewood was scarce and dear especially in the town, owing to the wasteful disafforestation that had been going on for centuries, and there were no peat bogs in the land. The olive, fig, vine, and fruit trees were generally spared. Other trees, like the oak, larch, pine, and the like, were seldom allowed to attain their full growth, but were ruthlessly cut down when young. Their foliage was given to the goats, the timber was sold to the carpenters and builders, and the lesser branches were made into charcoal. Only the twigs and sticks were used for fuel.[2] The word "coal," as found in the Bible, does not mean mineral coal, which was not mined in Palestine until the past century. Rather the word denotes charcoal, the making of which was quite an industry. That made from broom was preferred, as its thick roots gave off a stronger and more lasting heat.[3] The "fire of coals" at which St. Peter found the high priest's servants warming themselves was, of course, charcoal (cf. John 18:18). The richer people burned it in their ovens, for cooking, and in braziers to warm their rooms.

Poor people sent out their children to gather their modest meed of fuel for the day. "Seest thou not what they do in the cities of Juda, and in the streets of Jerusalem? The children gather wood, and the fathers kindle the fire, and the women knead the dough" (Jer. 7:17–18). Day after day, especially in winter, poor widows and the children roamed through the cold, wet fields searching for substitutes for good firewood. The prophet Elias saw the poor widow of Sarephta gathering sticks outside the gates of the city (cf. 3 Kings 17:10). This daily gathering of fuel, however, was forbidden on the Sabbath (cf. Num. 15:32). They would bring home anything that would burn, anything that would help to bake their daily bread and warm their shivering bodies: brushwood, stubble, briers, straw, or even thorns. "The Bible is a most accurate guide to the life of modern Palestine. Let me give an instance. I stopped at a humble little village. I do not know the name of it. There were some few

fields round about it, a well near it, and a baked mud road leading through to the flat-roofed houses and the little mosque. In
a clearing near the village several women sat beside a black pot
beneath which blazed the thorn bushes that grow all over
Palestine. As the thorns burned they made a crackling, splitting
sound, and I realised the descriptive power of that famous line
in Ecclesiastes: 'As the crackling of thorns under a pot, so is
the laughter of the fool' "[4] Weeds, stalks, the dried "grass of the
field," including the woody stems of such plants as the gladiolus
or anemone, "the lily of the field" of Palestine, were "cast into
the oven" (cf. Luke 12:27–28).

One of the commonest sights in Palestine is the line of
women out foraging for fuel and carrying home on their backs
and heads piles of thorny brushwood. On one occasion I saw
an angry Arab chasing some poor women out of his garden
in Bethany and fairly shrieking curses and threats at them, for
they had been stealing sticks and breaking branches from his
fruit-trees.

When these miserable substitutes failed, as they often did
in winter, the poorer families were compelled to fall back upon
the use of dung. The embers of the last fire were covered with
dung, previously dried in the sun, to make the next fire upon
which to bake their daily bread (cf. Ezech. 4:12). To this day
the Arabs of the desert make their cooking fires of camel-dung,
when there is no other fuel available. The children were sent
out to search the streets and highways. They carefully gathered
up the fresh droppings of animals and plastered it on the outside walls of their houses to dry. Nor is it necessary to go so far
abroad as Palestine to observe this custom. In some parts of
France, notably Brittany, the peasants use dung to augment their
scanty firewood. This form of fuel gives their bread a peculiar
flavour to which strangers find it difficult to accustom themselves.[5] One day, while wandering alone along the almost
deserted shores of the lovely Lake of Galilee, a poor Arab in-
vited me to break bread with him. We squatted on stones out-

side the door of his lonely stone hut, and his wife, her face heavily veiled in black against the gaze of the stranger, fetched out on a brass tray two cups of the inevitable treacly coffee and a thin flat cake as hard as a biscuit, and then retired within. The old Arab and I ceremoniously broke bread, and I shall never forget the pungent flavour of the first mouthful. For fear of offending my host I managed to overcome the nausea and bolt it down. It was my first taste of bread which had been baked on dung.

Joseph was one of the few inhabitants of Nazareth who did not have to depend upon substitutes for firewood. As a carpenter he had at his command an abundant supply of good firewood. In his workshop there were always superfluous pieces of wood, unused timber, splinters, shavings, and even sawdust. It is consoling to reflect that our Lady, as the wife of a carpenter, was not compelled to forage for fuel through the fields nor reduced to the use of noisome fuel in her oven.

Every family had its own oven, and Moses had predicted that in times of famine "ten women shall bake your bread in one oven" (Lev. 26:26), meaning that bread would be so scarce that one oven would suffice for ten families. These domestic ovens, not the fixed furnaces of the bakers, seem to have been of two kinds. One was a pot-like hole dug in the ground outside the building, owing to the danger of fire and the nuisance of smoke in the chimney-less houses. It was usually about three feet deep and two feet in diameter. The bottom was lined with stones upon which the fire was kindled, and the sides were coated with smooth plaster. The unbaked bread, formed into flat cakes of dough, was applied to the inside with a pad kept for the purpose or with the hand bound in a wet cloth.

The other domestic oven was a portable pot generally used inside the house, especially in inclement weather. It was about three feet high, broadening towards the base. The fuel was cast in through the top, which was then covered with a lid. When the fire within was hot enough, the flat strips of dough were applied to the outside of the pot until they were baked.[6] Jeremias said that the ardent pains of famine caused the skin to burn as an oven (cf. Lam. 5:10), that is to say, like the exterior surface of one of these heated pot-ovens. As the houses were chimney-less, the smoke escaped by day through the open doorway and by night through the window. This latter was little more than a small, unglazed aperture, grated and set high in the wall to be out of the reach of thieves and to ensure privacy. It was really more of a smoke-vent than a window, for the house during daylight was lighted by the open door and at night by the lamp.

Wax or tallow candles were not in general use, as vegetable oils, notably olive oil, were a product of the country and were cheap and abundant. The widow of Sarephta, poor as she was, had yet "a little oil in a cruse" (3 Kings 17:12). The word "candlestick" in the Bible is really a mistranslation for lampstand. Even the famous golden candelabrum of the Temple was really a seven-branched lampstand. The lamp in common domestic use resembled a tiny teapot in form, filled through a hole in the top and with a flaxen wick burning in the short spout. The museums have many specimens of these lamps of antiquity. The care of the domestic lamp, and more especially of the Sabbath lamp, devolved upon the woman of the house. The valiant woman is praised because "her lamp shall not be put out in the night" (Prov. 31:18). At dusk the lamp is lighted and it burns all through the hours of darkness, both for the purpose of a night-light and as a means to kindle the fire in the morning. The traveller by night through the countryside is surprised to see the number of lights shining from the dwellings. The reason is that the native, rich or poor, never goes to sleep without a light burning in his dwelling. No servant will stay with an em-ployer who refuses to allow him a night-light, for no one will sleep in the dark. The phrase "he sleeps in the dark" is used to indicate a person so destitute that he cannot afford even the price of a little oil.[7] Joseph, of course, as a respectable artisan in a booming trade could easily afford the trifling expense of a night-light, and Mary was too good a housewife ever to allow her lamp to be extinguished.

Thus Joseph, having closed the workshop and provided for the ass, found a warmed and lighted chamber awaiting him. The extreme simplicity of life in the East dispensed with the need of elaborate furniture. Most people dined off a tray, so they needed neither dining table, chairs, sideboard, nor even a dining room. Their beds were rugs and mats which were rolled up and put aside during the day, and so they did not require a separate bedroom. One room served readily for kitchen, dining room, and bedroom. So the furniture of Joseph's living-room was of the simplest. It consisted of the oven, the water-jars, the tray and its stool, the painted wooden chest made by his own hands and containing their Sabbath garments, the lamp, the spinning wheel, the kneading trough, some baskets, the wooden cups, platters, and bowls, some gaily striped cushions instead of chairs, the rolled-up rug and mats upon which they slept, and little more. There were no table knives or forks, for the people ate with their fingers, as did kings and queens until quite modern times.

Upon Joseph's entry Mary was seated on a cushion near the oven engaged in making swaddling clothes by the light of the lamp. The carpenter bowed to the Word made Flesh in his house before he sat down cross-legged beside her. He began to talk, while the winter rain drummed on the flat roof overhead, and the north wind, cold and raw from the snows of Mount Hermon, blew piercingly through the narrow streets. They heard the sharp barks of the pariah dogs outside, the scavengers of the streets, as they raced along seeking what they might devour (cf. Ps. 58:15), or growling as they quarrelled over the offal in the gutters. Joseph told Mary that he must obey the edict of Augustus. Much as he disliked leaving her alone under the circumstances, he was compelled to go to Bethlehem, for he dared not disobey the King's command. There was no need for her to leave home, for he could have his wife's name enrolled with his own. Besides, they were both descended from Jesse, the father of David and seven elder sons. Any man descended from one of these elder sons would be a member of the family of David. But Joseph was more; he was a direct descendant, not of any of the King's brothers, but of royal David himself, as the genealogies preserved in the Gospel prove. The evangelist states that Joseph was "of the house and family of David." So was Mary, for St. Paul expressly states that the Saviour was "of the seed of David, according to the flesh" (Rom. 1:3). Since the Saviour has no human father, His direct descent from David could be obtained only through His Mother "according to the flesh," so she was "of the house and family of David" too.

At first sight it may seem surprising to find members of the original royal family, the most illustrious in Israel and in whom the hopes of the future were founded, living quietly in a provincial town and earning their bread by the sweat of their brow. The dynasty of David had been dethroned by the Babylonians as long ago as 586 B.C., and since then his descendants had lived in obscurity. None of them came forward to play a prominent part even in the national resurgence led by the Machabees. It was the priestly House of Hasmon which obtained the crown and restored the monarchy for the brief century of independence preceding the rise of the House of Herod. The Davidites were content to remain private citizens until the Messias should be born of their seed. Other members of the family had migrated from Bethlehem and settled far away from the City of David. For example, in Babylon, beyond the frontiers of the Roman empire, the Jewish colony was ruled in domestic affairs by their "Prince of the Captivity," and he claimed descent from David through Jehoiachin, the last reigning king of the House of David. But in Palestine the Davidites remained in political obscurity, though socially they were the most distinguished family in Israel, and their genealogy was religiously kept, for everyone knew that the Messias was to be born of the House of David. In comparison with the old royal line of so many monarchs, the House of Hasmon was upstart and the House of Herod parvenu. It was in the home of "Isai the Bethlehemite" that David had been born and reared. Thus Bethlehem was the headquarters of the clan, and so Joseph had to go there from Nazareth for the census. His name was already inscribed there in the genealogy of the clan: now it had to be registered in the records of the State.

It is eighty-eight miles from Nazareth to Jerusalem by the modern, present-day road, and Bethlehem is six miles more. A "day's journey" was regarded as the unit of prolonged travelling. It was not only an indication of time but a real, though indefinite, measurement of space. Its length varied with circumstances; longer where the going was good, shorter where it was bad. There were no roads as such in the country until the Romans later began to build them. The primitive tracks which served as roads were sometimes partly obliterated by the winter rains and encumbered by boulders washed down by the mountain torrents.

The length of a day's journey also depended upon the capabilities of the traveller. The imperial courier, with relays at his service in every town through which he passed, could have put his twenty-five or thirty miles behind him in a day, while a large caravan, its speed regulated by the pace of its slowest animal, would do much less. The laden baggage camel usually proceeds at about 2½ miles per hour. There are about eight hours of daylight in a winter's day, but time must be allowed for loading and starting, the halt for the midday meal, and the unloading in the evening, which would total about fifteen miles daily for a camel caravan. Unencumbered travellers would do less than the speedy courier but more than the tardy caravan. Hence, for ordinary pedestrians, the average length of a day's journey in winter would be from twenty to twenty-five miles.[8] These facts were, of course, well known to Joseph. Unless impeded, he knew that he could walk to Bethlehem in four days. He did not know how long he would be detained there; one day at least, perhaps more, if many members of the clan arrived simultaneously and increased the work of the scribes. Then the Sabbath would intervene, a day upon which travelling was forbidden. Ten days or more might elapse before he would be back to Nazareth.

Mary listened, the needlework lying forgotten in her lap, with her eyes fixed upon the face of this young man, who in law was her husband and in fact was her best friend. The lamplight shone upon his lithe and slender figure in the blue tunic of the workman, upon his bronzed and healthy complexion, his brilliant but soft eyes, his black hair tumbling on his shoulders, his short beard. She listened, and once more from her heart rose up the prayer of gratitude to the Holy One, blessed be His Name, who had put her under the protection of this "just man," so considerate, so devoted beyond all thought of self. She had made her vow of virginity while still a girl in the Temple precincts. When she had left the Temple to come home to Nazareth, she determined to keep her vow, but she had to conform to the invariable custom of the country and become betrothed. Joseph would not have been accepted as her spouse if he had not agreed to respect her vow.

Mary remembered how troubled she had been when the angel announced that she was to become the Mother of the Messias. Even to the angel she had ventured to make her intentions clear. St. Augustine interprets her dialogue with the angel as her decision to keep her vow: "This is indicated by the words in which Mary answers the angel who tells her she is to bear a son: 'How,' she said, 'shall this be done, because I know not man?' She certainly would not have said this if she had not already vowed her virginity to God. But because Israelite custom did not allow for this, she had become betrothed to a just man, who would not take from her by force, but rather protect from violence, what she had vowed to God."[9] How confident Mary had been that Joseph would allow her to retain her virginity in the married state, and how perfectly that confidence had been justified since she had come to dwell in his house! Surely Joseph, like their ancestor David, was a man "after God's own heart," since God had trusted him so absolutely!

There was a pause while Mary pondered over Joseph's words. It was only a few months since she had crossed his threshold to enter his house as his wife. She loved every stone in this house of refuge, from the strong roof overhead to the rock foundation beneath her feet. He was like his house: safe, strong, and secure. But she loved him more than his house and she would not be parted from him in her hour of need. Since he had to go to Bethlehem, she would go with him. She would endure the discomforts of the journey rather than be separated from the just man into whose care she had been committed by God. Now she tells him so, and he bows his head, overwhelmed by this signal proof of her trust and love. Besides, Mary added, there was another reason, to her mind a compelling reason, why she should go to Bethlehem. The prophet Micheas had foretold that the Messias would be born in Bethlehem. Reverently she recited the inspired words so familiar to her by constant meditation since the Word had become Flesh: "And thou, Bethlehem Ephrata, art a little one among the thousands of Juda: out of thee shall he come forth unto me that is to be the ruler in Israel" (Mich. 5:2).

Mary would go to Bethlehem so that there her days might be accomplished. Joseph had said that they must render obedience to Caesar. Mary obeyed all the more willingly because she felt that Caesar was only the instrument of the divine plan. She looked upon the inspired oracle of the prophet as a divine command which she was bound to obey. After this there was no more to be said. The fireside conference was over. Joseph abandoned his intentions in favour of hers. To the difficulties of his long winter journey he would add the burden of a woman in delicate condition. A burden? It was rather a privilege and a joy to have her accompany him. Together they knelt down for their night prayers. Soon they would leave Nazareth — for a much longer time than they anticipated. Little did they dream that they should have to cross the desert and flee into Egypt before they would see their home in Nazareth again. That night they added to their prayers the prayer prescribed for going on a journey. How marvellously it would be answered the future would show! Here is the same prayer in the modern form which is still in use:

"May it be thy will, O Lord our God and God of our fathers, to conduct us in peace, to direct our steps in peace, to uphold us in peace, and to lead us in life, joy and peace unto the haven of our desire. O deliver us from every enemy, ambush and hurt by the way, and from all afflictions that visit and trouble the world. Send a blessing upon the work of our hands. Let us obtain grace, loving kindness and mercy in thine eyes and the eyes of all who behold us. Hearken to the voice of our supplications; for thou art a God who hearkenest unto prayer and supplication. Blessed art thou, O Lord, who hearkenest unto prayer.

"And Jacob went on his way, and the angels of God met him. And when Jacob saw them, he said, This is the camp of God: and he called the name of that place Mahanaim (a double camp). Behold, I send an angel before thee, to keep thee by the way, and to bring thee into the place which I have prepared. The Lord bless thee, and keep thee: the Lord make his face to shine upon thee, and be gracious unto thee, and give thee peace."[10]

CHAPTER 6

Making Ready for the Road

COCKS were the clocks of ancient Palestine, for there were no mechanical timepieces. Our modern system of reckoning the day from mid-night to the following mid-night, a custom adopted from the ancient Romans, was not followed by the Jews and Greeks, whose day began at sunset and ended at the next sunset. For example, the Sabbath began at sunset on Friday evening and ended at sunset on Saturday evening, a reckoning observed by orthodox Jews to this day. The method of reckoning the hour differed also: for us an hour is invariably sixty minutes, but in Palestine its duration varied. Night was divided into four watches and daylight into twelve hours. This appears evident from the question addressed by our Saviour to His disciples: "Are there not twelve hours in the day?" (John 11:9.) The first hour began at dawn, when the owner of the vineyard found labourers waiting to be hired in the market place (cf. Matt. 20:1). The third hour would correspond with our 9:00 a.m., the sixth with noon, the ninth with 3:00 p.m., and the eleventh was the hour preceding sunset. Thus it was daylight, rather than the day, which was divided into twelve hours, summer and winter, and the sixth hour was always noon. Hence the length of the hour varied with the duration of daylight. In mid-summer an hour was about seventy-five minutes duration, and in mid-winter only forty-five, though at the equinox it was sixty minutes. "All the hours are not equal," said Rabbi Joshua. These varying hours are still alluded to in such expressions as *horae astivae*, the "hours" of the Breviary, prime, terce, sext, none, and the like.[1]

In New Testament times the night was divided into four watches, each of three hours, varying in duration according to the season of the year. These four watches are mentioned in the text: "Watch ye therefore (for you know not when the lord of the house cometh: at even, or at midnight, or at the cock crowing, or in the morning)" (Mark 13:35). The evangelists record the fact that on Holy Thursday evening the Saviour warned St. Peter that he would deny Him thrice before the cock crew, and St. Mark has the significant variation: "Before the cock crow twice, thou shalt thrice deny me" (14:72). It is difficult to fix a definite time for the first cock-crowing, as cocks crow at irregular times from midnight onwards, but the second was the cock-crowing proper which announced the break of day, the time at which the rabbis prescribed the following Benediction to be recited: "Blessed art Thou, O Lord our God, King of the Universe, who givest understanding to the cock to distinguish between day and night."[2] At the instant of dawn the cocks roosting on the flat roofs of the town roused the sleepers below with their discordant din as effectually as alarm clocks.[3] Even the household of the high priest in Jerusalem was awakened by the chorus of cock-crowing from the barns and stables in the outer court of the palace.

> The cock, that is the trumpet to the morn,
> Doth with his lofty and shrill-sounding throat
> Awake the god of day.

The cluster of white houses on the hillside of Nazareth was still dim in the darkness of a winter's morning when the cocks began to crow and awaken the sleepers to another day. The people sat up in their beds and recited the prescribed Benediction. What a quaint morning offering! The women arose, took down the night lamp from its bracket on the wall, used its faint flame to kindle the fire in the oven, and then extinguished it. The men hastened to open the outer door and admit the pale light of the dawn. Soon the narrow lanes were filled with women, pitcher on head, hurrying down for fresh water. The yawning watchman unbarred the massive gates to let them out to the well. When the light was bright enough to distinguish between the colours blue and white in the sky, or if overcast, on the fringes of the mantles of the men, it was the hour for morning prayer. These prayers are mentioned in the following ordinance of the rabbis: "Women, slaves and little children are exempt from the recitation of the Shema, and from the Phylacteries, but are under obligation in the case of The Prayer, and the Mezuzah, and the Blessing after Meals."[4] The phylacteries were a kind of amulets or protection cases, consisting of two tiny leather boxes containing texts, one for the head and one for the arm. So Joseph donned his phylacteries, turned his face south towards Jerusalem and the Temple, the abode of Jehovah on earth, and sat down to recite the Shema, for sitting was the position prescribed. The *Shema* was a kind of creed or profession of faith in the God of Israel. It consisted of three passages taken from the *Pentateuch,* or *Torah* as it was called, namely Deuteronomy 6:4–9; 11:3–31; Numbers 16:37–41.

Then Mary returned with her pitcher full of fresh water. The prayer to be recited while washing was: "Blessed art Thou, O Lord our God, King of the Universe, who removest sleep from mine eyes and slumber from mine eyelids."[5] Standing was the position prescribed for the recitation of The Prayer, so Mary and Joseph arose to their feet, faced south towards the Temple, and said it aloud together. It was a long prayer, consisting of the Eighteen Benedictions.[6] There was neither holy picture nor statue in their home in Nazareth, although today there are representations of Mary and Joseph in every Catholic home throughout the world. The prohibition of graven images by the First Commandment was so strictly interpreted that no picture or statue of living things was permitted, lest the people be seduced by the beautiful conception of Greek art and lapse into the idolatry of their heathen neighbours.

Hence, too, the warning against idolatry contained in the *Shema,* and the absence of images of living things on the coins. The Hasmonean priest-kings had minted shekels bearing the device of the flowering lily or the chalice in addition to the lettered inscription. They did not presume to stamp their own heads on their coins. The heathen coins from the mint at Tyre bore the effigies of the gods, of course, and the Roman coins were stamped with the head of Caesar. These coins were regarded as idolatrous and were not accepted in the Temple. They had to be exchanged for the shekels and half-shekels of the Hasmonean dynasty. Herod issued coins bearing only such innocent emblems as an anchor, a tripod, a cluster of grapes, a cornucopia, or a helmet. Only at the end of his reign, when he had broken with the Pharisees, did he venture to flout public opinion by minting a coin with the device of the eagle, the symbol of imperial Rome. So there were no pious pictures or statues on sale in the Temple repositories, and the walls of the homes of the people were bare of sacred art, although the houses of their heathen neighbours were full of images of the gods and the graceful statuary of the Greeks.

After Mary and Joseph said their morning prayers on the day of their departure for Bethlehem, Mary baked the day's supply of bread and they ate their ordinary breakfast of hot, fresh bread washed down with spring water. They had neither tea nor coffee, and it was not usual to drink wine so early in the day (cf. Acts 2:13, 15). Did they have any other food at breakfast? They could have had fish, which was cheap and abundant, owing to the proximity of the great Lake of Galilee. When the Apostles returned to the shore after a night's fishing, they made their breakfast of bread and fish (cf. John 21:9). They might have eaten an egg, for bread, fish, and eggs were the commonest articles of food and are enumerated in the triple question of the Saviour (cf. Luke 11:11–12). Because it was winter, there were no fresh fruits or vegetables available, but they could have had some dried fruit, either figs or dates or olives. And, of course, they would eat a good breakfast to sustain them for the journey.

Bread, however, was the principal constituent of every meal; other things were regarded as accessories. In the East bread is the staff of life, so much so that the word bread, *lehem,* could mean bread in particular or food in general, "our daily bread." When the ploughman, sower, vinedresser, or fisherman left his house for his day's labour, or the pilgrim, pedlar, or traveller started on his journey, he wrapped any other food he may have had in the thin loaves of bread baked that morning in the oven. It was bread alone that the man asked from his neighbour to put before an unexpected guest. "Which of you shall have a friend, and shall go to him at midnight, and shall say to him: Friend, lend me three loaves, because a friend of mine is come off his journey to me, and I have not what to set before him" (Luke 11:5–6). Two of the flat loaves would have made an ample meal for one person, but traditional hospitality demanded that abundance be set before a guest. When the loaves are fresh they are soft and flexible, but they harden rapidly and are then broken like the modern biscuit. Hence the expression, "the breaking of bread," denotes having a meal (cf. Luke 24:35).

Bread was usually made of wheat flour. It is true that bread was also made of barley; for example, the multiplication of the loaves was wrought upon "five barley loaves" (cf. John 6:9). Barley, however, was principally grown as fodder for animals, and was eaten only by the very poor people. For example, it was barley which was bestowed upon poor Ruth (cf. Ruth 3:15). "Barley bread is only eaten by the poor and unfortunate. Nothing is more common than for these people, at this day, to complain that their oppressors have left them nothing but barley bread to eat."[7] Mary was neither poor nor unfortunate, and so her bread was made of wheat flour.

Bread was eaten with gratitude as a gift from God, and the

grace pronounced over it was: "Blessed art Thou, O Lord our God, King of the Universe, who bringest forth bread from the earth." It was also regarded with reverence. "In a land where communication with other sources of supply was difficult, everything depended upon the local wheat and barley harvest. As this in turn depended upon the rain in its season, which was beyond the control of the sower, a special sanctity attached itself to what was peculiarly a gift of God, and a reminder of His continual and often undeserved care (Matt. 5:45). To the disciples of Jesus, 'Give us this day our daily bread,' would seem a very natural petition. An Oriental seeing a scrap of bread upon the road will usually lift it up and throw it to a street dog, or place it in a crevice of the wall or on a tree branch where birds may find it. It should not be trodden underfoot in the common dust. Thus the most familiar article of food, so constantly in the hands of all, both rich and poor, and used alike by the evil and the good, had in it an element of mystery and nobility as having been touched by the unseen Giver of all good. How deeply this feeling of reverence possessed the mind of the Lord Jesus is evidenced by the fact that He was recognised in the breaking of bread."[8] And now Mary and Joseph are preparing to journey to Bethlehem, literally "The House of Bread," a name due to the fertility of its fields and the excellence of its wheat. In Bethlehem will be born the Saviour who will give His flesh and blood to be eaten under the form of bread and wine.

They set about providing food and clothing for the journey. "Take with you victuals for a long way" (Jos. 9:11), was the advice of the ancients. They would bring that day's bread with them and no more, for they could buy fresh, hot bread each morning from the ovens of the bakers in the towns through which they passed. They would bring no meat with them, for meat was a comparative luxury. They would have a skin "bottle" of wine and a jar of oil, like the Good Samaritan on his journey (cf. Luke 10:34). Palestine was indeed "a land of oil" (Deut.

8:8), and the importance of its olive oil can scarcely be over-estimated. It was used for light, soap, cooking, medicine, and massage. At about this time Herod himself was taking oil baths in the hope of healing his disease.[9] "In ancient times generally (and in many places at the present day) the olives were ground to a pulp in huge stone basins, by rolling a heavy stone wheel over them, and the oil was then expressed in stone presses established near by. Frequently these presses, with their floors, gutters, troughs, and cisterns were all hewn out of solid rock, and thus literally 'poured out rivers of oil,' as Job hath it in his parable. There is a ruin above Tyre, near Kanah, called Im-il-Awamid, where scores of such presses are still standing, almost as perfect as they were twenty centuries ago, though every vestige of the groves which supplied the oil has long since disappeared."[10] No wonder that Moses spoke of "oil out of the hardest stone" (Deut. 32:13). The word Gethsemani has been interpreted to mean "oil-press," and it was in the Garden of Gethsemani that the Saviour began to pour forth His precious Blood for the redemption of mankind. Mary and Joseph would pack a jar of oil for their travelling lamp, for Mary was no "foolish virgin" to be without oil when she needed it most.

How much money would Joseph require for the journey to Bethlehem? The answer to this question would depend upon the cost of living. Fifty years previously the daily wage for a labourer was half a drachma, so it is presumed he could live on that. The great Hillel, who rose to be the most illustrious of the jurists, came in his youth from Babylon to Jerusalem and worked as a labourer for half a drachma a day.[11] On this sum he was able to support himself, his wife, and infant son, and apparently also to pay the fees for admission to the lectures in the Academy. His son, Simeon, would be older than St. Joseph, and his grandson was the illustrious Gamaliel, at whose feet Saul of Tarsus was proud to sit as a student of the law, and who defended the Apostles before the Sanhedrin. But in the New Testament times the standard wage of the labourer had risen to

Mount Ebal and the ancient town of Sichem
from Mount Garizim

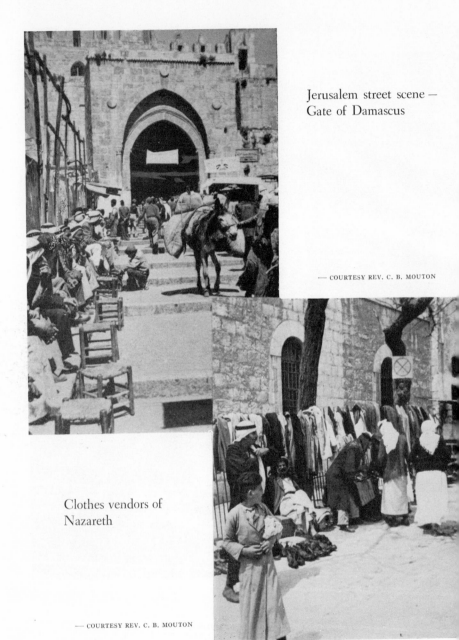

Jerusalem street scene —
Gate of Damascus

Clothes vendors of
Nazareth

a whole drachma per day, as we learn from the parable of the labourers in the vineyard (cf. Matt. 20:2).* From the historian Tacitus we learn that the daily pay of the private soldier was the same, one drachma or denarius.[12] We may conclude, therefore, that the cost of living for the rural worker did not exceed a drachma, and that this sum would be sufficient for the daily expenses of the journey to Bethlehem.

There was no car fare to pay, for there were no cars, as wheeled traffic was impossible without good roads. Provender for the ass would not cost more than a trifle. Mary and Joseph needed money only for food and lodging, and not so much even for that, for a host, with the traditional hospitality of the East, would be just as likely to refuse all remuneration. The journey would take at least four days each way, not including the enforced rest on the Sabbath. If Mary's days were accomplished while she was in Bethlehem, as she hoped and believed, they would have to remain there for about ten days. So twenty drachmas would be amply sufficient for the journey. But they foresaw another expense. The Mosaic law prescribed that a first-born son should be ransomed from the service of the

---

*The drachma was the standard Greek coin of commerce in use throughout the entire eastern Mediterranean. Judas the Machabee collected twelve thousand drachmas for sacrifice in the Temple for those who had fallen in battle (cf. 2 Mach. 12:43). The drachma was the "groat" lost and found by the woman in the parable (cf. Luke 15:8). It was a silver coin issued from the mints of Antioch, Tyre, and Caesarea, and bore devices differing according to its date and place of issue. The best known was the Attic drachma, which spread over the East after the conquests of Alexander. It bore on its obverse the head of the goddess Athene and on the reverse her emblem of the owl, and at this time weighed 55 grains troy.

The denarius, weighing 60 grains, was the standard silver coin of Rome and was the only legal silver coin in the western half of the empire. In the eastern half, however, the system based on the Greek drachma was retained. It was the famous "coin of the tribute" (Matt. 22:19), bearing on its obverse "the image and inscription of Caesar," and on the reverse a female figure, probably representing the Empress Livia, holding a sceptre and a bough. It is misleadingly translated as a "penny." It was with two of these denarii that the Good Samaritan paid the innkeeper's bill for attendance on the wounded Jew (cf. Luke 10:35). The denarius was worth a trifle more than the Greek drachma.

Sanctuary by a payment of five shekels, that is, twenty drachmas.
They would bring that sum with them and fulfil the law when
returning through Jerusalem.

What was the salary earned by Joseph by the sweat of his
brow as the bread-winner of the Holy Family? During the thirty
years of peace under the rule of Herod the country rose to unprecedented heights of prosperity, so much so that the King
was able to extract vast sums in taxation without impoverishing
his subjects. "St. Joseph lived at a busy time for carpenters,
masons, and the rest, for the reign of Herod inaugurated a
golden age of building in Palestine. This parvenu among princes
had a truly Napoleonic passion for architecture, and surpassed
even the fame of Solomon as one of the great builders of
antiquity. He expended much of his enormous wealth upon
sumptuous structures which gratified his love of pomp and
display, and he left his mark all over the land by erecting
palaces, fortresses, theatres, hippodromes, public baths, and
gymnasiums according to the prevailing fashion in Greek culture. The feelings of the orthodox among his subjects were
outraged by many of his foreign innovations, but gratified by
his rebuilding of the Temple of God. Besides, the great harbour
works of the new port he built at Caesarea enhanced the
prosperity of all his subjects, Jew and Gentile alike. There is
not a hint in the Gospel that St. Joseph was ever employed
in the grandiose building works of the King, and it is unlikely,
for he lived in out-of-the-way Nazareth, far from the great marts
of trade and centres of culture. Nevertheless he must have
profited by the boom in building caused by the King's passion
for architecture, for the magnates and rich men of Galilee would
be stirred to emulate the King and follow the prevailing fashion.
From all this it can be inferred that there was constant employ-
ment and good wages for craftsmen of all kinds."[13]

Another indication of the wealth of Palestine is that the
Temple treasury contained cash equal to 2000 talents and gold
of the value of 8000 talents more, when Crassus plundered it.

All this money had been contributed by the piety of the people "out of their abundance" (Mark 12:44). This treasure of ten thousand talents was worth 2,400,000 gold pieces, even if the talents were only of silver. The fact that the gold fell to half its value after the siege of Jerusalem is a further proof of the prosperity of the country before A.D. 70. St. Joseph could earn much more than the drachma per day of the agricultural labourer. He was a skilled artisan in a booming trade, whose services were in constant requisition and were richly remunerated. Hence he could easily afford the forty drachmas for the expenses of the journey to Bethlehem and for the anticipated offering in the Temple.

What clothes would Mary and Joseph require on the journey? The costume of both sexes was much the same, for breeches do not seem to have been worn except by the priests and by them only during their weeks of duty in the Temple. Dress consisted of five articles: namely, tunic, head-dress, girdle, mantle, and a pair of sandals. The tunic was a close-fitting, sleeved undergarment like a shirt except that it was long enough to reach the feet. Men engaged in their work usually girded up the tunic in front so as to leave the legs free. It was made of linen for summer-wear and wool for winter, and was usually white in colour. The girdle was either a leather belt with a buckle or a woven sash of brightly dyed cotton wound several times round the waist—this latter would be worn usually by women. St. Peter had his tunic—unfortunately translated as "coat"—thus girded about him while fishing (cf. 21:7). A man clad only in his tunic was conventionally said to be naked.

The head-dress of men is never explicitly mentioned in the Gospel, though the napkins binding the heads of the Saviour and Lazarus in the tomb may well have been their head coverings in life (cf. John 11:44; 20:7). No one would dare go out in the summer sun without his head being protected from the heat and his eyes from the glare. Hence, modern pictures of our Saviour and His disciples going about bareheaded do not correspond with reality. The head-dress worn by men of the period cannot have differed much from the present *khefieh*, a loose cloth hanging down on the neck and shoulders and bound round the head with a short, black rope called the *agaal*. Women wore a light veil in summer and a heavy shawl in winter. Besides, it was considered undignified to leave the head bare, and so it was kept covered even indoors. It was not the head-dress which men removed on entering a dwelling, but their sandals, lest they bring in the mire of the streets upon a clean floor. To this day Moslems leave their shoes outside the mosque before they venture upon its holy ground. Christians, when they are admitted to a mosque, are not required to remove their shoes, but are provided with big, clumsy overshoes. When, for example, the slim, young sheik of the Mosque at Hebron personally conducted the author around, he stepped daintily in his socks across the richly carpeted floor, while I shuffled awkwardly beside him in awful overshoes which felt as big as boats. To this day the Jews keep their heads covered in their synagogues.

The cloak was the fifth article of apparel and completed the costume. This cloak was the ample outer mantle, the largest and heaviest garment of all. It was worn as a protection against cold and rain, and also as a kind of full dress. "This is made of camel's or goat's hair or of wool, and among the fellahin [peasants] is usually of white and brown in stripes or of plain brown. The superior qualities are often white or black. The ordinary aba [mantle] is made of a long rectangular piece of material, with the sides folded in and sewn along the top; it is thus very square, when new, across the shoulders and the upper arms. It extends half-way between the knees and the feet. During sleep, especially on journeys when the traveller has no bed, it is made to cover the whole person, the man either wrapping it round him, or, if there is a sack or mat on which to lie, curling himself under it as under a blanket."[14] This elaborate mantle would require the art of a tailor, though the other garments were usually made by the women of the household.

The tunics worn by Mary and Joseph were made by the Blessed Virgin herself. She was so proficient that the seamless tunic of her Son was of such quality that His executioners were unwilling to cut and divide it, and so cast dice for it (cf. John 19:23–24).

The clothing seems to have been made without pockets. The lower part of a man's tunic was commonly drawn up to his knees and tucked in above the girdle. The upper part formed a receptacle called "the bosom" (cf. Luke 6:38), in which various small articles could conveniently be carried. The Saviour enumerated the usual items of equipment for a journey when sending out His disciples on the mission tour of Galilee: "And he commanded them that they should take nothing for the way, but a staff only: no scrip, no bread, nor money in the purse, but to be shod with sandals, and that they should not put on two coats" (Mark 6:8–9). These particular instructions applied to this tour only and were later revoked by the Saviour (cf. Luke 22:35), as they obviously could not be fulfilled by disciples setting out for foreign climes and distant lands. A man familiar with the customs in the Orient thus interprets the particular instructions for Galilee: "Provide neither silver, nor gold, nor brass in your purses. You are going to your brethren in the neighbouring villages and the best way to get to their hearts and their confidence is to throw yourselves upon their hospitality. At this day the farmer sets out on excursions quite as extensive, without a para in his purse; and the modern Moslem prophet of Tershiha thus sends forth his apostles over this identical region."[15]

Mary and Joseph were not undertaking a missionary tour, and so such precepts would not apply to them. They would bring the normal equipment of travellers. The scrip mentioned in the Scripture passage was the wallet, a bag made of partially tanned kid skin, carried by a strap from the girdle or slung over the shoulder. This was David's "shepherd's scrip, which he had with him" (1 Kings 17:40), and in which he carried his provisions. Mary and Joseph would carry well-furnished wallets for the journey, from which they could refresh themselves as they rested by the wayside or in the shelter of the inn at night. It was the custom for those on a journey to bring "two coats," that is, two tunics, a necessary change of underlinen. The staff, of course, was the ordinary walking stick of the East, rather longer than ours, a stout, slightly tapering rod, serviceable for support or for defence against thieves or wild beasts. Mary would also have one to support her steps while walking, for she would become too numb if she rode all the time at the slow pace of the ass. The purse was a little bag made of leather or cloth, usually suspended from the neck by a thong. Also it could be carried in "the bosom" or attached to the girdle outside.[16] In this purse Joseph carried his money for the journey. Since Herod had repressed organised brigandage a sword would not be as necessary as it became in later and more turbulent times (cf. Luke 22:36, 38).

It was the custom for the women of the period to cover their hair as evidence of their modesty before men, and for men to cover their heads as a sign of their reverence before God. It seems that young girls and children were allowed some laxity in the privacy of their own home, but it was the invariable rule for both girls and married women to cover their heads in public. It was the mark of a sinner in the city, a shameless one, to go about with her hair uncovered. A married woman who appeared bareheaded in the street was considered to have put her husband to shame and was liable to be divorced. The distinction of the lady Kamhit, who had the honour of seeing several of her sons attain to the dignity of high priest, was attributed by the rabbis to the fact that she was always so careful in keeping her head covered that "the ceiling of her house had not seen the hair of her head."[17] St. Paul, too, insists that Christian women, even of Gentile stock, should keep their hair covered during divine service (cf. 1 Cor. 11:13). Mary would always wear her veil or shawl in public, like any other modest matron.

Joseph allowed his beard to grow, for shaving was forbidden by the law of Moses (cf. Lev. 19:27; 21:5). Hence the Israelites were distinguished by their beards from the earliest times. In the Assyrian monuments Asiatics are always represented as bearded and Egyptians as shaved. Therefore the first Joseph was shaved before being presented before Pharaoh (cf. Gen. 41:14). But even the shaved Egyptians wore artificial beards on state occasions. On the monuments subjects are represented as wearing short, artificial beards, kings with long ones, and the gods with beards longer still, being curled at the points. Even Queen Hatason, by reason of her rank, is depicted on her monument as wearing an artificial beard. Chaldea was the place of origin of the Hebrews, for Abraham came from there. On all the Chaldean monuments only women and eunuchs are portrayed as beardless. To cut off a man's beard, either in whole or in part, was a serious insult. The Ammonites shaved off half the beards of David's ambassadors, who hid themselves in Jericho in shame until the half-shaved beard grew again. David considered this insult to his representatives such a deadly affront that he waged war on the Ammonites (cf. 2 Kings 10:2-5; 1 Par. 19:2-5). The rabbis said that "the adornment of a man's face is his beard."[18] The so-called Apostolic Constitutions prohibited shaving "as being contrary to nature and as changing the form of man." It was the custom to perfume the hair and beard with oil at banquets and state occasions (cf. Luke 7:46). There is no explicit mention of beards in the Gospel, but the general tradition, supported by the evidence of the monuments, is that the Saviour and His Apostles wore natural beards. The sole exception is St. John, who is represented as a beardless youth. The normal age for a man to marry was eighteen.[19] At that age Joseph's beard was just growing. Beards have always been held in high esteem among Semitic peoples as the crown of manhood. Modern Arabs say they would consider themselves less disfigured by cutting off their nose than by shaving their moustache. Hence, they are inclined to look with contempt upon the clean-shaven Christian.

CHAPTER 7

Crossing the Plain

ONE day I noticed an interesting family group coming in from Bethany to the market in Jerusalem: a peasant, his wife, his child, and his donkey. They reminded me of the Holy Family only by contrast, for it was the man who rode. He sat at ease on the donkey, twirling his moustache and looking languidly about him, with his legs dangling almost to the ground, while the poor woman trudged patiently in the dust behind him. The wife carried the child on her hip and a heavy basket of vegetables on her head, while her lord was unencumbered. She was not even allowed to walk beside him, but was compelled to walk in the rear, the proper place for women. Nor would her husband condescend to speak to her in public, except to issue his commands. The man was a Moslem, of course, and among Moslems there is no such thing as equality of sexes. To them a woman is little better than a household drudge or beast of burden. Such sights are rather a shock to Christians, but such occurrences are common enough in the Orient. It was consoling to remember that Mary and Joseph did not travel thus, for the Chosen People had a higher notion of the dignity of women. For example, Moses, returning to Egypt, put his wife and their two children upon the ass while he walked (cf. Exod. 4:20). The true believers were happy to follow the example of their great law-giver. Besides, Joseph was aware of the sublime dignity of Mary — and of her condition — and so he would not dream of compelling her to walk while he had a beast for her to ride.

The Scriptures indicate that the ass was the usual mount of both sexes, both rich and poor. Besides Moses, we read of the prophet Balaam riding an ass (cf. Num. 22:21); Axa, the daughter of Caleb (cf. Jos. 15:18); Abigail, the wife of the churlish Nabal (cf. 1 Kings 25:20); Achitophel, the king's counsellor (cf. 2 Kings 17:23); Miphiboseth, the son of King Saul (cf. 2 Kings 19:26); and the thirty sons of Jair rode thirty ass colts (cf. Judges 10:4). "When it is said that Christ is 'lowly,' because He should ride on an ass (Zach. 9:9), compare Matthew 21:7; the reference is not to any degradation in the riding of an ass, but to the peaceful nature of His advent. The horse was used in war, and a king coming upon a horse would be surrounded by military circumstance and pomp. Asses are still ridden by persons of rank in State and Church. There are many fine breeds of them, and every large city of the interior boasts its special strain. Many of these are sold at very high prices. They have a rapid walk, and an easy shuffling pace or short canter. They are exceedingly sure-footed. Some of them are breast high, and weigh as much as a small horse. White asses (Judges 5:10) fetch specially high prices, and are very handsome beasts, while their caparisons are often quite magnificent. These consist of a thick stuffed saddle, often covered with crimson, or dark green, or other rich coloured cloth, bound with braids of brighter colours, and with silver ornaments and dangling tassels of woolen twist. The headstall and bridle are likewise decorated with shells, silver studs, and plates, and not infrequently composed in part of silver chains. A collar of silver links, with a breastplate of the same metal, complete the adornment."[1]

Tradition has it that our Lady rode to Bethlehem on an ass. On the morning of their departure the neighbours of Mary and Joseph assembled to see them off. The ass, made ready for the journey, stood outside the door on the wet cobblestones of the narrow street in the half-light of the early winter morning.

Joseph helped Mary mount, and she rode side-saddle, for etiquette did not permit women to ride astride unless in exceptional circumstances.[2] What a pretty picture Mary must have made, as she sat upon her gaily caparisoned donkey! Her long white tunic under the brown mantle of warm goat-hair reached to her feet, her head and shoulders muffled in her shawl of blue and white stripes, her beautiful face blushing like a rose in the cold air of the morning and with the natural excitement caused by the adventure of the journey, for we should remember that she was only sixteen at the most. There she sat, "The Lily of Israel," surrounded by her women friends, all wishing her a safe journey and a speedy return.

Joseph then locked the door of his house which, if he only knew it, he was not to open again for many months, not weeks. The type of lock of the period was of wooden construction, usually of walnut or mulberry, and, in this case, probably made by Joseph himself. "The Syrian lock consists of two pieces of wood set at right angles to each other. The upright piece is nailed to the door, and has in its upper part four or five holes bored, into which headed pins, or nails with the points cut off, are dropped; the upper part is then plugged with wood. When the cross-bolt is pushed rapidly into the socket in the door-post these pins fall into holes made in the bolt to receive them, and so prevent its withdrawal. The bolt is hollow from the outer end for rather more than half its length, and into this hollow end the key is inserted. The latter is a piece of wood about 9 in. long, with pins inserted in its upper surface at one end, to correspond with the holes in the bolt. When the pins in the key enter the holes in the bolt, the key is pressed upwards, and the pins of the lock are thus raised above the bolt, which is then set free, and is withdrawn by the key. The length of the bolt is usually about 8½ in., but there are locks very much larger. The key, owing to its size, is generally stuck in the girdle, but is sometimes tied to a handkerchief and slung over the shoulder."[3]

There is a reference to the cumbrous wooden keys, large enough to be used as clubs defending their property, in the text: "And I will lay the key of the house of David upon his shoulder" (Isa. 22:22). David and Solomon were the ancestors of Joseph, but instead of their palace he occupied a humble house in Nazareth. He locked his door and withdrew the huge key, confiding it to the care of a neighbour. Then he took his staff in one hand and, grasping the bridle in the other, led the donkey down the street. They were off!

At the gateway the watchman stifled his yawns and respectfully wished a safe journey to the Son of David. They emerged from the close, dark streets out into the open air and the freshness of the morning. Passing the well on their left, they descended the hillside upon which Nazareth was built. They passed through the vegetable gardens and groves of bare olive trees which encircled the town, then through the stony fields beyond until the ground rose again. About a mile from the town the chain of hills which surround Nazareth terminate abruptly in two peaks, separated from each other by a deep and narrow gorge. The more western peak is now known as the Mount of Precipitation, for tradition identifies it with the brow of the hill from which the Nazarenes tried to cast the Saviour down headlong (cf. Luke 4:29). From this precipice there is a sheer drop of about 900 feet. The view is magnificent from the summit of this mount, for the Plain of Esdraelon stretches away into the dim distance. It seems as flat as a billiard table and as uniformly green, except where chequered by brown fields where the plough had turned up the raw earth. Leaving the twin peaks behind them, the holy couple descended into this level and fertile plain.

The summer and autumn had gone by since Mary had travelled this route on the return from her visit to Elizabeth. Six months' drought had dried up the land. The Palestinian farmer never has to worry that rain will spoil his harvest; he can, in autumn, gather in his crops without any of the anxieties that beset our farmers, for "rain in harvest" in Palestine is as phenomenal as "snow in summer" (cf. Prov. 26:1). But the long spell of dry weather also has its disadvantages. The grass is burnt up, the streams disappear, the rivers shrink to a comparative trickle, and the water stored in cisterns evaporates. The ground is baked hard as iron, and dust can be a blinding nuisance. When the east wind blows in from the desert across the sweltering Jordan valley, the temperature can rise to as much as 105 degrees Fahrenheit, and it drops but little during the short nights. A cup of cold water in summer is no trifle, but a most welcome and refreshing gift.

After the long drought, heavy and continuous rain is much needed, not only to swell the streams and rivers, but also to saturate the parched earth down to the roots of the trees and enable the husbandman to begin his ploughing and sowing. "Let us fear the Lord our God, who giveth us the early and the latter rain in due season: who preserveth for us the fulness of the yearly harvest" (Jer. 5:24). Delay in the coming of the rain can be a calamity. The early rains begin in October and usually come down heavily. The latter rains usually finish up in March. Between the two there is more or less continuous rainfall with intervals of bright weather. The saying that "it never rains but it pours" is quite applicable to Palestine. "The rain and the snow come down from heaven, and return no more thither, but soak the earth, and water it, and make it to spring, and give seed to the sower, and bread to the eater" (Isa. 55:20).

Tropical heat and sunshine are popularly associated with the climate of Palestine, but they do not prevail all the year round. Furthermore, the climate varies in different parts of the country and at different altitudes. There is torrid heat in the Jordan Valley, at its lower end no less than 2000 feet below the level of the Mediterranean, for it is the deepest trench in the world; at the same time people on the hills of Jerusalem, 2610 feet above sea level, are enjoying mild weather, while Mount Hermon, more than 7000 feet higher, maintains cold, alpine climate.

Winter begins in December, and the month can be both cold and wet. One author thus describes a typical winter's night: "It was the 3rd of December, too, and a winter storm was coming on in all its might and majesty. Lightnings blazed along the mountain-tops, and heavy thunder bellowed through the wadies of the upper Owely. As evening advanced, the wind began to sob and groan among the rocks and trees, and vast volumes of black vapour, rolling in from the sea, settled on the heights of Lebanon like a 'horror of great darkness.' The long-expected and much-desired rains had commenced."[4] With such weather as this in December, no wonder our Lord advised His disciples: "But pray that your flight be not in the winter" (Matt. 24:20). Yet, by the edict of Caesar, His own Mother and foster-father were compelled to travel during this inclement season.

As Mary and Joseph descended into the great Plain of Esdraelon, they could see the ploughmen at work all around them. These unfortunate peasants had to wait until the land was thoroughly softened and saturated by rain before their primitive ploughs could even scratch the surface. The ploughs were of a simple kind that had not altered since the days of Abraham. They were usually made of wood and tipped with iron, having a light beam and an erect handle. Some were drawn by oxen and some by asses, but ox and ass were never yoked together: "Thou shalt not plough with an ox and an ass together" (Deut. 22:10). The ploughman held the handle in his left hand, and urged on his reluctant beasts with the goad in his right. He did not look about him nor behind him, for he had to concentrate all his attention on his work. With an inattentive driver the beasts might default, or the plough merely scrape the surface or knock against the stones and rocks that encumbered the fields. This illustrates the text: "No man putting his hand to the plough, and looking back, is fit for the kingdom of God" (Luke 9:62). The Chosen People were forbidden to have bullocks, so the oxen at the ploughs would be scrub bulls or cows (Lev. 22:24). Palestinian cattle were puny and weak compared with the carefully bred monsters nourished on our grazing lands. The goad was not a whip, but a sharply pointed stick, and its application made the poor brutes kick. "It is hard for thee to kick against the goad" (Acts 26:14).

Doctor Thomson's descriptions of Palestine are particularly valuable, for he wrote a hundred years ago, when the country was still under the rule of the Turk, and conditions were much the same as they had been from time immemorial. Concerning ploughing, he says: "I am surprised to see the plain covered with men ploughing and sowing at this late season. This is common and will continue all winter. It has always been so, I suppose. Solomon says: 'The sluggard will not plough by reason of the cold, or "winter," as the margin has it; therefore shall he beg in harvest and have nothing.' Our farmers do actually plough in the severest weather. I have often seen them shivering with cold, and contending with wind and rain, quite enough to discourage those who are not sluggards. But time has become precious and critical, and he who expects to reap must sow, no matter how tempestuous the weather. . . . This hard necessity of winter-work is mainly owing to the wretched implements used, and to a strange deficiency in agricultural science and skill. If the farmers had good ploughs and adequate teams, they might break up and prepare their ground in fair weather, and then, when sufficient rain had fallen, they would sow the whole crop in a few days. But these men, with their frail ploughs and tiny oxen, must wait until the ground is saturated and softened, however late in season that may be. They cannot sow and plough in more than half an acre per day, and few average so much, and hence the work is dragged along for months. They know nothing about the harrow, and merely plough under the seed, and leave it to take its chance. Job, however, speaks of the harrow; and if our translation be correct, it is one of the oldest agricultural implements in the world."[5]

The fields are not fenced, and many little paths, beaten hard by the passage of many feet, meandered through them. As the teams of ploughmen were goading their wretched cattle up and down in the rain, Mary and Joseph would pass close by them. They would see, too, the sower scattering the precious seed from a basket. In winter the prevailing wind blew from the west and was laden with the moisture of the Mediterranean. On a windy day the seed would be blown broadcast. Flocks of birds followed the sower — crows, pigeons, larks, and the ubiquitous sparrows. Even the seagulls came screaming inland for their share. No wonder tears were the lot of the hapless sower when he saw so much of the good seed wasted, devoured by voracious birds, when it could have been made into bread to feed his hungry children: "Going they went and wept, casting their seeds" (Ps. 125:6). Mary and Joseph, wending their way slowly through the field paths, did not escape the wind and the rain, for it "raineth upon the just and the unjust" (Matt. 5:45).

By midday Mary and Joseph would have reached Jezreel, about ten miles from Nazareth. The town was built upon a hill rising about 200 feet above the level of the surrounding plain. Jezreel means "God Soweth," a tribute to the fertility of the land. Here King Achab had built his summer palace, and the wisdom of his choice is proved by the strength afforded by the hill and the extensive and beautiful view from this central location. To the west rolls the immense plain until shut in by the bushy heights of Mount Carmel in the distance; to the north the bold bluffs of Mount Gilboa rise from the level; to the east the mountains of Galaad arise beyond the Jordan, and to the south the eye roams over the green expanse to where the hills of Samaria rise into the sky. The track from Nazareth and the north ascends gently through the bare trellises of the vineyards to the walls of the town.

The lounging gatekeeper, sunning himself in the pale winter sunshine, saw the man, woman, and donkey coming up the path. They seemed so ordinary that he barely gave them a second glance, and his response to Joseph's greeting was merely mechanical. They did not enter the town, but skirted the walls to the east for nearly another mile to the famous spring. Besides the advantages of its site, Jezreel possessed the further benefit, as inestimable as it was rare, of an abundant supply of excellent water. The spring gushed from the rock, forming a limpid pool of forty to fifty feet in diameter which was full of fish. Mary and Joseph halted here for rest and refreshment. Here was the traditional scene of David's victory over the giant Goliath, an event which roused the fighting spirit of the people against their oppressors, the Philistines, and was the prelude to many victories. According to Josephus, it was at this beautiful pool that Achab had Naboth and his sons stoned to death and the dogs licked up their blood, and afterwards the blood of Achab himself, when his blood-stained chariot was washed at the pool. His infamous Queen, Jezabel, was hurled down from a window of the palace, and her proud flesh was eaten by the dogs.[6] After the fall of the House of Achab the glory of Jezreel decreased and its name is mentioned no more in sacred history.

The dog is mentioned over forty times in Scripture and always with contempt. This could not mean the shepherd's dog, which watches over the fold at night and attacks prowling wolves and jackals, nor the domestic dog, employed in guarding houses and tents. It can refer only to the masterless pariah dog of the streets. These seem to have been omnipresent in New Testament times and to have made the nights hideous with their barking. They spent much of their time, when not in search of their carrion food or biting one another, in sleeping under the shelter of walls and vaulted passages or sprawling in the mud and dust of the streets. They were looked upon as the type of everything unclean, cowardly, treacherous, and idle.[7] These pariah dogs seem to have been exterminated, for they are not seen in present-day Palestine.

The dogs of Jezreel had a reputation for savagery: "There have ever been in all the cities and villages of the East, troops of hungry and half savage dogs, which owe allegiance to no one, but tenaciously maintain their rights to a particular and generally very limited district, within which they will never permit the dogs of the adjoining village or street to enter; and who wander about at night, the only scavengers, clearing away carcasses and offal of every kind, which but for them might create a pestilence. Even human graves, unless well secured, are not safe from their search. . . . On the very spot on the mounds of Jezreel, outside the modern hovels, as Dean Stanley remarks, and as the writer has often seen, the descendants doubtless of these very dogs may be seen searching for refuse. . . . It is from this habit of these uncared-for outcasts, as well as from its being ceremonially unclean, that the dog is almost always in Scripture spoken of with more or less aversion and contempt. In every language of the East the term dog is applied as a name of scorn or reproach. . . . As the Jews contemptuously applied the term 'dog' to the Gentiles, so to the present a Mohammedan will rarely speak of a Christian without the epithet 'Dog.' 'Dog of a Jew,' 'Dog of a Christian,' are expressions rarely out of his mouth."[8]

It was natural for Mary and Joseph to rest under the palms at the Pool of Jezreel where they could break bread in peace and refill their water "bottles." The dogs prowled around, of course, for the pack that haunted the mounds around the Pool would scent the strangers and come snarling around for a share of their meal, or even to attack them if feasible. But Joseph's staff, wielded by his strong arm, would repel them to a respectful distance. Then, having performed the ablutions prescribed by the law, broken bread with thanksgiving, reposed themselves a while and cared for the needs of the patient ass, they arose and continued the journey, this time up towards the orchards of Engannim, ten miles away.

Soon they left the level plain behind them, and the path ascended towards the mountains of Samaria. When the wounded Ahaziah had fled from Jehu, this ascent was too rough and steep for his chariot, so he drove around by the level land to Megiddo, where he died (cf. 4 Kings 9:27). Engannim, still flourishing among the gardens from which it derives its name, is situated at the head of a valley leading up from the plain. The adjoining hills are covered with plantations of olives and figs; the houses are surrounded by gardens separated from each other by cactus hedges. The town itself is fenced by a wall of cactus whose stems are so huge and whose spikes are so interwoven that passage through it would be impossible if openings had not been cut in this living rampart. The source of this luxuriant growth is a spring, or rather torrent, which flows down from the hills into the valley, there divides into many streams, fertilises the gardens and orchards, and diffuses an agreeable coolness in the height of summer.[9] These brooks would be full after the winter rains when Mary and Joseph arrived, and the place melodious with the sound of running water.

In Palestine the temperature drops suddenly at night, making the winter evenings very cold. Although they could rest by the spring in the open air at midday, Joseph would be solicitous to seek shelter for Mary at night. The natural and obvious shelter in a strange town is the inn. There must have been many of these in the Palestine of the period. In ancient days, when the Hebrews were a pastoral people and travelled in caravans with their flocks and herds, they did not need inns. But since they had become an agricultural people, tilling their fields and tending their vines and fig trees, and with a large commercial class in their dense population, inns on the high-ways became a necessity. Also the volume of traffic from Asia to Europe, and from Alexandria to Damascus and Antioch, passed along the land route through Palestine, and paid toll at the customs stations. St. John enumerates some of the articles imported into Rome by the merchants of the earth in the first century, many of which he must have seen borne along the highways of his native land. "Merchandise of gold and silver, and precious stones; and of pearls, and fine linen, and purple, and silk, and scarlet, and all thyine wood, and all manner of vessels of ivory, and all manner of vessels of precious stone, and of brass, and

of iron, and of marble. And cinnamon, and odours, and oint-
ment, and frankincense, and wine, and oil, and fine flour, and
wheat, and beasts, and sheep, and horses, and chariots, and
slaves, and souls of men" (Apoc. 18:12–13). Herod's new port
of Caesarea would deal with many exports from the East.

The inn of the ancient East was very different from a modern
hotel. It provided shelter, not entertainment, for man and beast,
and hence its construction was of the simplest. It had neither
kitchen nor dining room nor bedroom nor waiter nor chamber-
maid. Its walls were built to provide travellers, in the old days
of insecurity, with protection and shelter from the weather, and
no more. It was usually a rectangular building of one story,
built on rough stone. It had no windows and only one entrance,
the gate. Inside the gateway was the courtyard, open to the
sky. Here the travellers tethered the beasts and piled their bales
of goods. Around the courtyard was the *leewan,* a broad platform
raised a foot or two above the level of the yard, and roofed over.
It was usually divided into alcoves or compartments, absolutely
devoid of furniture. Here the traveller rested for the night. They
provided their own food and bedding, attended to their own
wants and cattle. The innkeeper was merely the man in charge
who kept the peace, allotted the places to travellers, and collected the fee.

On cold, wet nights the beasts, if untethered, would try to
scramble up to the shelter of the *leewan.* European travellers
have complained bitterly of the appalling discomfort and of the
lack of privacy in the alcoves, which they were compelled to
share with all and sundry, including the insects. "And there in
the midst of that confused jumble of men and animals, some
haggled and bargained while others prayed to God, some sang
while others slept, some ate and others relieved themselves; a
man might be born and another might die, all amidst that filth
and stench with which the encampments of traveling Beduins in
Palestine still reek even today."[10] Those arriving when the
platform had been filled had to take their place among the

donkeys, camels, and bales of goods in the yard below. But anything was better than exposure to the wintry night in the open and the danger from prowling beasts and predatory men. So the traveller was content to pay a trifle for the advantages of safety, shelter, and a place to lie.

It was still daylight when Joseph helped Mary dismount in front of the gate of the Engannim inn, and was pleased to see that there was room for them. Having paid the customary copper or two, they were allotted a recess upon the platform. Joseph unbound the saddle with its caparisons and laid all on the stone floor. Then he provided for the needs of the donkey and tethered it in the yard below. Meanwhile, Mary spread out the padded cushion and the rugs which, during the day, formed the saddle and, at night, were used as bedding. She opened the wallet and took out the bread, wine, and dried fruit for their supper. Then she got ready the water and towels for the ablutions prescribed by the rabbis.

Before Joseph returned, Mary had time to look about her. It was an animated scene. The ground below was occupied by other travellers settling down their beasts for the night, while in the alcoves opposite she could see others preparing their meals. As darkness drew on, the travellers lighted their lamps as they settled down to eat. The place was full of sound: the voices of men and women, the grunting of camels, the munching of donkeys, the barking of the watch-dog at the gate. Suddenly there was an uproar. Some pariah dogs had sneaked in under cover of darkness and were driven out by blows of the inn-keeper's staff. She was glad when Joseph returned and seated himself on the rug beside her. Their simple meal was soon eaten, and their prayers said while the night was still young. It would be very unlikely that they would travel this much fre-quented road without meeting some acquaintance, and so the remainder of the evening, perhaps, was spent in gossiping and story-telling, for most Orientals are very sociable and dearly love a long gossip.

CHAPTER 8

Over the Hills

AT COCKCROW Mary and Joseph were astir again, for the next stage was long and they did not wish to waste any of the eight precious hours of daylight. The whole of the day's journey lay through the province of Samaria, and the natives were as hostile to Jews as they dared to be under the stern rule of Herod.

They wended their way up and down the hills and across the rich upland plains between the mountains, through fields where cattle and sheep were grazing, along hillsides terraced with figs and vines and olives, through the forests and thickets of that prosperous province. They had bought bread for the day in a bakery in Engannim, for they feared to enter a Samaritan shop. So they hastened on, never entering a town but skirting its walls, casting apprehensive glances at the inhabitants working in the fields. In years to come the Samaritans will refuse hospitality to the Saviour and His Apostles, who were obviously going up to Jerusalem on pilgrimage. "And they received him not, because his face was of one going to Jerusalem" (Luke 9:53). This rebuff awakened the old sectarian bitterness in the hearts of James and John, and they wanted to call down fire from heaven upon this Samaritan town.

At midday Mary and Joseph halted. They would choose a secluded place by the wayside where they would not likely be

seen or molested by the natives. But it was improbable that they
passed through the whole province without some manifestation of
hostility. The boys of Bethel would not let a stranger pass
without insult. We recall what had happened to the prophet
Eliseus. "And he went up from thence to Bethel: and as he
was going by the way, little boys came out of the city and
mocked him, saying: Go up, thou bald head. And looking back,
he saw them, and cursed them in the name of the Lord: and
there came forth two bears out of the forest, and tore of them
two and forty boys" (4 Kings 2:23–24). Mary and Joseph could
not always escape the attention of parties of children foraging
for fuel, who would consider it a work of religious zeal as well
as a congenial pastime to deride any passing Jews. So it could
easily happen that as they rested by the wayside they would be
surrounded and mocked by these little wretches, who would
yell out, "Go up, thou dog of a Jew!" or "Go up, thou perfectly
accursed!" which seems to have been their favourite name for a
true believer.[1] And, of course, the instinct of such little villains
would be to pelt them with stones from a safe distance. So
Mary and Joseph would be compelled to rise and hurry on until
the boys tired of the sport and desisted. Under the Old Law of
fear the insult to Eliseus was avenged, but at the dawn of the
New Law of love Christ the Lord and His own endured such
things patiently.

After midday they approached the capital of the province,
Sebaste. At this time the city was inhabited, not by the Samaritans, who after all were only schismatics or heretics, but by Gentiles, who were worse, being outright idolaters. At the sight of
idolatry in Israel every true believer would recite the prayers
prescribed by the rabbis: "He that seeth idolatry says: Blessed
is He who is slow to anger. He that seeth a place from which
idolatry was uprooted says: Blessed is He who hath uprooted
idolatry from our land; may it be pleasing in Thy sight, O Lord
our God, that idolatry be uprooted from our land, and from
all places in Israel, and mayest Thou turn the hearts of them

that worship idols to worship Thee."[2] The site of the city was
beautiful. "Samaria or Shomeron in the vernacular is derived
from the Hebrew word for 'pertaining to a watch' or 'a watch-
mountain'; and we should be almost inclined to think that the
peculiarity of the situation of Samaria gave rise to its name.
In the territory originally belonging to the tribe of Joseph, there
is a wide, basin-shaped valley, encircled with high hills. In the
centre of this basin, which is on a lower level than the valley
of Shechem, rises a less-elevated oblong hill, with steep yet
accessible sides, and a long flat top. This hill was chosen by
Omri, as the site of the capital of the kingdom of Israel."[3] Hence,
the city was founded nine centuries before Christ, and had a
chequered history.

As recently as 107 B.C. the city had been besieged and taken
by the Hasmonean Priest-King Hyrcanus, who set about uproot-
ing heresy by destroying the city. More recently, in the turbulent
days of Herod's rise to power, the inhabitants of the district furnished him with war supplies. It was in this friendly town that
Herod celebrated his nuptials with Mariamne, the lovely Hasmonean princess, and the inhabitants sheltered his family when
he himself was compelled to flee to Rome. When he returned
triumphant over his enemies he remembered his friends by
rebuilding the city on a grander scale. Besides, the strategic
advantages of the site were as plain to Herod as they had been
to King Omri, the founder long before. The hill of Shemer commanded two main routes, one from the south and one from the
east. These converged at Sichem, and then divided again to
run northwards and westwards just south of the city itself. The
site was easy to defend, being surrounded by valleys on all sides.
The inhabitants, not being Jews, had shown themselves favour-
able to Herod, and he saw the advantages of creating here a
central stronghold and of populating it with people devoted to
his interest. He surrounded the hill-top with a new circuit of
walls, two and a half miles long, and fortified them with towers.
He also built a new forum and a stadium or sports grounds. On

the summit of the hill he constructed a new temple with a spacious esplanade. This he dedicated to Augustus, his imperial patron, and re-named the city Sebaste, the Greek for Augusta. Nor did he neglect the local cult. The favourite deity of the inhabitants was Kore the Maiden, a goddess of the underworld like the Persephone of the Greeks. Her shrine was close to the new temple of Augustus but on a lower level. This, too, Herod embellished and enlarged. This setting up of idolatry in Israel must have been a grievous affront to his Jewish subjects. But the King reinforced the friendly natives with six thousand of his discharged veterans and their wives and families, and gave them allotments of the best land in the district.

Nowadays Sebaste is in ruins. The hill-top, one of the most famous places in the Bible, is inhabited only by a few wretched Arab families, who follow the visitor around begging for *baksheesh* or proffer him coins and bits of mosaic for sale. Recent excavation has unearthed one of the round towers of the city wall, the esplanade of the temple of Augustus, and some pillars of the forum and stadium. But the visitor today, standing on the steps of the temple built by Herod, can survey one of the most interesting views in Palestine, and see below him the path followed by Mary and Joseph on their way to Bethlehem for the first Christmas.

In their time, of course, Sebaste was at its zenith, a proud city set upon its commanding hill, surrounded by its shining new wall and with the gleaming columns of the temple of Augustus towering over its roofs. Mary and Joseph would not, dare not, enter the pagan town. They passed beneath the hill to the east on the way to Sichem. The veterans working in the fields and allotments would be sure to shout ribald remarks after the Jew and Jewess hurrying past with eyes averted from the seat of idolatry. The road wound along for another six miles until it reached the town of Sichem. The name means "shoulder" or "ridge," for the town was situated on the side of Mount Garizim. On account of its situation as midway between Galilee and Judea it was also called Mabortha or "thoroughfare."[4]

As it was customary to make the journey between the two provinces in four stages, travellers found it convenient to halt at Sichem on the second night.[5] It was one of the loveliest as well as one of the most sanctified spots in Palestine. It lay in a sheltered valley, with Mount Ebal on the north and Mount Garizim on the south not more than 500 feet apart. The bottom of the valley is 1800 feet above sea-level and Garizim's summit is 800 feet higher still. "The whole valley was filled with gardens of vegetables, and orchards of all kinds of fruits, watered by fountains which burst forth in various parts and flow westward in refreshing streams. It came upon us suddenly like a scene of fairy enchantment. We saw nothing to compare with it in all Palestine. Here, beneath the shadow of an immense mulberry tree, by the side of a purling rill, we pitched our tent for the remainder of the day and the night. . . . We rose early, awakened by the songs of the nightingales and other birds, of which the gardens around us were full."[6] In this noble vale Abraham had pitched his tent and had built an altar to the one true God. It was here that Jacob had dug his famous well and that the tomb of the first Joseph had been built. However, when Mary and Joseph arrived, Sichem had long been the stronghold of the schismatic Samaritans. Here on Mount Garizim they had built their temple in rivalry to Jerusalem. One day the Samaritan woman will say to the Saviour: "Our fathers adored on this mountain, and you say, that at Jerusalem is the place where men must adore" (John 4:20). At Jacob's well the same woman will be astonished to hear Him ask her for a drink of water: "How dost thou, being a Jew, ask of me to drink, who am a Samaritan woman? For the Jews do not communicate with the Samaritans" (John 4:9).

It was only too true. The Jews opprobriously designated the Samaritans as "Cutheans" (cf. 4 Kings 17:24), that is, being of mongrel origin, and the rabbis declared: "Let no man eat of the bread of the Cutheans: for he that eateth their bread is as he that eateth swine's flesh."[7] For a Jew to eat pork was to put himself outside the law. One day the Saviour will treat the Samaritans with tenderness, but His hour is not yet come. It is one of the freaks of history that while the Jewish priesthood and Temple have long since come to an end in Jerusalem, the despised Samaritans have clung to their site on Mount Garizim and have retained their hereditary priesthood. The fall and destruction of Jerusalem in A.D. 70 put an end to the national state and church of the Jews in Palestine, and so it is nearly nineteen hundred years since sacrifice has been offered in Jerusalem by a Jewish high priest. The Samaritans have remained; they still celebrate the Passover sacrifice on Mount Garizim and have had a line of high priests down the centuries.

Today the Samaritans number only 260, but they are still there. It is true that the Jews have come back to Palestine, driven out the natives, and have even set up a new state of Israel. But the Arabs have succeeded in keeping them out of the old city of Jerusalem, and the site of the Temple remains in Moslem hands. They are excluded even from their Wailing Wall. One of the strangest scenes I saw in the Old City was that of little Arab children playing hop-scotch in the Street of the Wailing Wall, where generations of Jews have mourned for their departed greatness. The present High Priest of the Samaritans received me graciously in his house in Nablus below Mount Garizim. He is a tall, brown-faced, hawk-nosed aristocrat, and looks as if he had just stepped out of the pages of the Old Testament. He claims descent from Aaron the first high priest — a pedigree of nearly 3000 years. He allowed me to handle the famous manuscript of the Samaritan Pentateuch written on lambskin and enclosed in a silver case, which is probably one of the oldest surviving manuscripts of the first five books of the Bible.

Mary and Joseph would not be welcome in the town of Sichem, so they would not venture inside the walls nor buy the legally impure Samaritan bread. They would prefer to

seek shelter for the night outside the town and consume the
provisions they brought with them. They could take refuge
under the foliage of a sycamore. This tree was usually planted
near the wayside, for its long, nearly horizontal branches project
over and shelter the passing traveller. It should not be confused
with the tree known by the same name in Europe and America.
The Eastern sycamore is of the same genus as the fig tree and
is known to botanists as the *Ficus Sycamorus*. It is always
verdant, even in winter, and affords shelter all the year round.
It was easy for Zacheus, the little publican, to climb into it from
the wayside and see the Saviour passing below (cf. Luke 19:4).
Seated on one of the lower boughs would be within easy speak-
ing distance of the Master.[8]

From ancient times men sought out trees under which to rest:
Abraham under the oak of Mambre (cf. Gen. 18:4) and Elias
under a juniper in the wilderness near Beersheba (cf. 3 Kings
19:5). Under the protection of the giant branches of a sycamore
Mary and Joseph could find some comfort for the night, the dry
saddle-cloths spread between them and the ground and covered
by their warm mantles of goat hair. The ass could be tethered
close by. In winter bears descended from the snowy heights of
Hermon and Lebanon to the woods and thickets of the valleys
and plains, like the bears who avenged Eliseus at Bethel near by.
Lions, too, prowled by night, but they would not approach too
near to a city. These must have been very numerous in ancient
times, for the Bible is full of references to them. At one time
there was such a plague of lions in Samaria that the people peti-
tioned the King of Assyria to deliver them (cf. 4 Kings 17:26).
It is only since the twelfth century that lions have become extinct
in Palestine. But neither lion nor bear, unless extremely hungry,
attacked human beings without provocation; their ravages were
confined to flocks and herds. Of course, pariah dogs prowled all
night, but their barking was so familiar to Mary and Joseph
that it did not disturb them. If the beasts came too near, then
Joseph would rise and beat them off with his staff.

The rising sun awakened them to the third day of the journey. They said the beautiful morning prayers with their faces turned towards Jerusalem, now so much nearer. Any one of the abundant springs of the noble vale provided them with plenty of fresh water for their ablutions. After eating their simple morning meal, they left Mounts Ebal and Garizim behind them and descended into the extensive plain of Mucnah, dotted with villages and girdled by hills. Here the fields were already full of people busy with the winter sowing. Soon the path began to ascend, for they were now "going up" across the mountains of Ephraim towards Jerusalem.

It was most difficult going up and down the rocky tracks on the hillsides, but Joseph was young and able for it. In the steeper places Mary could dismount and walk with her hand on the saddle as the surefooted ass picked its cautious steps among the loose stones of the declivities. They gave way and stood aside when meeting larger parties of travellers on the narrow track, especially if any of these happened to be heathens, as the Law forbade all contact with such. Caravans as a matter of course took the crown of the causeway. Picture Mary and Joseph stepping off the road when they saw a caravan for Damascus, for example, topping the rise in front of them. The merchant-owner on his donkey rode in advance. Then came the string of laden camels, each supercilious head on its reptilian neck bobbing and swaying over the vast rump with its tiny tassel of a tail of the beast ahead of it, with the great wide feet padding silently along to the jingle of a bell dangling from each neck. The owner cast indifferent eyes on the humble couple by the wayside, and his servants and spearmen had the news of the day to gossip about as they trudged along on foot.

As time wore on the journey must have been increasingly difficult for Mary in her cramped position on the donkey's back and exposed to wind and weather. She would dismount at times and walk a while where the going was easy on the upland plains among the mountains. This, of course, would help to restore the circulation and warm her cold limbs. But in her condition she could not walk for very long. She would have to resume her seat on the saddle and submit to be buffeted by the gusts of cold air which rushed unobstructedly down the mountains, often bringing with it icy winter rains. Her thick shawl and her goat-skin mantle helped to keep her warm and dry, but they were not impervious to continuous rain. It was too fatiguing to sit upright for long without any support for the back, so she would lean upon Joseph's sturdy shoulder. He was the man chosen by almighty God to protect and sustain her, and she could depend upon him with the utmost confidence.

There exists an ancient carving in ivory, dating from as long ago as the sixth century, which originally formed one of the panels decorating the ivory throne of the Exarch of Ravenna. The cunning hand of the pious artist has depicted in touching fashion the dependence of Mary upon Joseph in this weary journey. An angel is pictured as leading the donkey by the bridle and holding a lighted candle before the Word made Flesh. To Joseph is allotted the more honourable duty of supporting the drooping form of the Mother of God. Her right arm encircles his neck and she reclines upon his shoulder. She appears to be suffering, but her attitude expresses absolute confidence in the strong man who so tenderly sustains her. He walks along with his eyes cast down and with the expression of the most reverent affection.[9] In some such fashion as that portrayed on this charming ivory of antiquity Mary and Joseph wended their way over the hills of Ephraim.

Another difficulty of the journey was the lack of bridges. The word *bridge* is mentioned only once in the Bible, and even in this solitary instance it may not refer to a fixed bridge at all but to the earthen rampart of a city (cf. 2 Mach. 12:13).[10] There probably was no permanent bridge over any river until later when the Romans began to build roads and bridges. There was little need of them in the long summer months, when every river in the country, except the Jordan, dried up in the fierce heat and left a dry bed which could be crossed on foot. But in winter, during the heavy rains, all these wadies or water-courses filled up again and became foaming torrents, pouring down from the mountains. How, then, did the people cross the rivers in winter? They were compelled to make detours along the bank until they reached a ford — a place where the water was shallow enough to permit crossing on foot. Hence fords were important landmarks. There were two principal fords across the Jordan, one opposite Jericho for crossing into Moab, and the other at Betharaba, where St. John the Baptist is said to have baptised the people. "Some of the fords of the Jordan, of which about forty were identified by the Palestine Survey, are impassable in spring or early summer, as the waters swollen by the melting of the snows of the Lebanon and adjoining regions rise and overflow their banks, covering the alluvial plains on either side."[11]

The Wadi Yatma formed part of the boundary between Samaria and Judea. Joseph was careful to seek a ford shallow enough to permit the passage of Mary high and dry upon the donkey. He would not risk a ford where a strong current might sweep the legs from beneath the donkey, so his search was long and painstaking. The water was icy cold, of course, and Mary must have shivered as she beheld Joseph splashing through, with his right arm held firmly around her, and his left gripping the bridle of the donkey. When they finally did cross over, they stood upon the sacred and friendly soil of Judea.

CHAPTER 9

Approaching Jerusalem

THE "hill country" of Judea is rightly so called, for this part
of Palestine has as its characteristic scenery rounded hills, broad
valleys, rocky soil, terraced vineyards, stretches of wilderness.
This was the original settlement of the tribe of Juda: here the
"Lion of Juda" made his lair. In the conquest of Canaan the
tribe of Juda smote the heathen hip and thigh and settled down
in the region to which they gave the name of their ancestor.
Nor could they be dislodged from their mountain lair. David
was hunted like a partridge on these grey hills (1 Kings 26:20),
but eventually he made Juda supreme among the twelve tribes.
Later the tribes of the north and west were swept away by the
Assyrian kings; Galilee and Samaria will soon be conquered by
Romans. Juda will be the last to succumb, and with her down-
fall will perish the national state and church.

Mary and Joseph saw more vineyards in Judea than in Galilee
or Samaria, but the vines were bare and leaf-less at this season
of the year. If the hills of Judea were bleak, its wine was the
best. The strips on the hillsides were terraced for the vine, the
vineyards were defended by walls and watch-towers, and the
wine-presses of stone were everywhere. It was in the Judean
valley of Eschol, "the Ravine of Grapes," that the spies cut down
the gigantic cluster of grapes which required two men with a
pole to transport it (cf. Num. 13:24), and the vines of Eschol

are cultivated to this day. The Prophet Isaias represented the Kingdom of Judea under the figure of a vineyard: "My beloved had a vineyard on a hill in a fruitful place. And he fenced it in, and picked the stones out of it, and planted it with the choicest vines, and built a tower in the midst thereof, and set up a winepress therein: and he looked that it should bring forth grapes, and it brought forth wild grapes" (5:1-2). Hence the vineyard of "the man of Juda" was destroyed (5:7). The Saviour will compare the kingdom with a vineyard, of which the tenants will kill the Son of the Lord of the vineyard, and so be brought to an evil end (cf. Matt. 21:33). Thus the vine was the symbol of the nation: it was stamped on the coins of the Machabees, and Herod hung a colossal cluster of golden grapes over the porch of the Temple.

Soon after crossing the Wadi Yatma the path which Mary and Joseph followed ascended once more and wound through the hills until it reached a bare and bleak plateau. Behind them, if they turned to look, the view was magnificent; the wide plain below, beyond it the massive mountains of Ebal and Garizim, and, if the day was clear, they could see Mount Hermon raise its snow covered head into the northern sky. But Joseph's face was set as of one going up to Jerusalem, and he did not look back. Below them lay another plain, girdled with hills and dotted with villages. The rocky hillsides were whiter than elsewhere, but the soil was rich and nourished many vineyards. The town of Beth Laban had the distinction of being one of the five towns which furnished the wine for the Temple libations.[1] On the other side of the hill, to their left, was the town of Kerioth, the birth place of Judas Iscariot. They next passed by the town of Beth Laban, known as Lebona in the Bible (Judges 21:19), surrounded by its vineyards.

A short distance beyond Beth Laban the terrain ascends once more. Here there was an inn and a well, where they would pause, allowing Mary to rest, for the next ascent was very steep. The inn today has been turned into a police station of the

The tomb of Rachel, located near Bethlehem

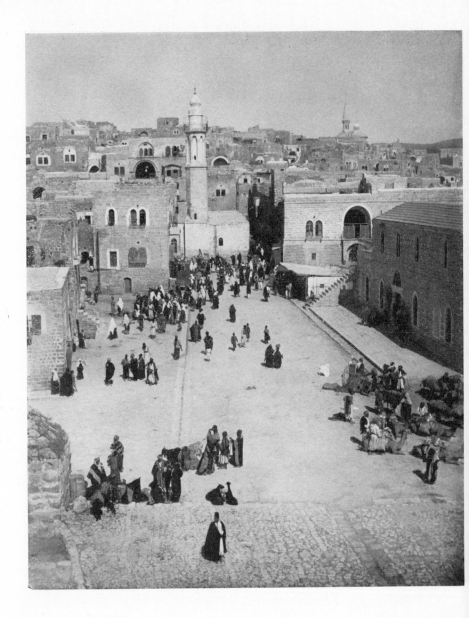

The bazaar of Bethlehem

Arab Legion, and the track has become a modern road which ascends the steep hillside in a series of hairpin turns which compel the motorist to go up in low gear. But in ancient times there was neither motor car nor road, but only a rough, steep track which must have been a strain on the lungs and legs of Joseph. Mary mounted again to lean upon his shoulder while he urged the ass forward and upward. They toiled wearily up the zig-zag track, one of the steepest on their route, with the loose stones slipping beneath them. They must have been relieved when they reached the summit at last and saw another valley lying below. It was known as the Valley of Oil, for the flanks of the surrounding hills were terraced and densely planted with olive trees.

Soon they entered a long, narrow gorge on either side of which arose high rocks pitted with caves. This was the key of the route between Sebaste and Jerusalem, and, of course, had been the haunt of robbers in unsettled times. The gorge was known as "The Eyes of the Robbers" from the fanciful resemblance to eyes of the caves high up in the rocky sides. From these eyries the robbers spied on the road, swooped down to rob and murder in the narrow pass, and then retreated with their spoils to their lairs above. Many a hapless traveller had been stabbed here in the gloomy gorge, despoiled of his wallet and clothing, and left to stain the stream with his blood. But the incidents of murder and rapine had decreased considerably, for organised brigandage had been outlawed by Herod. Mary and Joseph passed safely through the defile, meeting nothing more formidable than other peaceful travellers or a shepherd leading his flock to the spring that bubbled out of the rocks by the wayside. Halfway through the pass there was an inn on their right beside the spring and a small fort on the opposite side of the way. The soldiers of the King not on duty lounged in the inn and drank wine in the wineshop. It was now getting on toward dusk, and the lamps were lighted. Mary and Joseph saw the soldiers squatting on the floor, engaged in their favourite pastime of shooting dice, with the light shining redly on their armour. They were foreign mercenaries, Gentiles, but their presence was a guarantee of the preservation of the peace.

It was dark in the gorge, but it was lighter outside where the path widened out into the Valley of Oil again. Mary and Joseph would spend their third night at the inn of Beeroth, a few miles farther on. They were glad to be near a friendly town once more and away from the bigotry of the Samaritans and the hostility of the Gentiles. Beeroth means "wells," as there was abundant water, and the town is only about ten miles north of Jerusalem. It stands just below the ridge which bounds the prospect north of the Holy City. It was the first place at which caravans were accustomed to halt when travelling northwards. Here Mary and Joseph would find shelter and not be compelled to spend another night in the open.

It is possible that when Mary and Joseph emerged from the gorge and saw the wide open sky, they could see that a storm was imminent. Winter tempests in Palestine are frequent and sometimes terrible. "It was on the 28th of December. Some friends of mine, from Hasbeiya, were coming down the hill by Kefr Keely, that village west of Matully, when one of them called their attention to tall columns of mist over the marsh of the Huleh. They came this way very rapidly, and soon broke upon them with awful fury. Those of the party who were from Khyam, on the east side of this plain, fled homeward. My friends were driven before the blast to Khureibeh, that little hamlet just north of us, and with difficulty escaped to it. Those who attempted to reach Khyam perished in the plain, although it is not more than two miles wide, and in full view of their houses. Thus ten men died in a few minutes from the mere chill of this wonderful wind. There was no snow, no frost, and not much rain; but the wind was perfectly awful, driving and upheaving everything before it. These cold winds draw out all animal heat with amazing rapidity. Not only were these men chilled to death almost instantly, but eighty-five head of cattle also perished before they could be brought to the village. The inhabitants have no tradition of a similar catastrophe. People often perish in snow-storms on the mountains, and on the vast desert of the Hauran; but it was never known before that a mere wind, and that down on this low plain, could chill people to death. . . . I examined into the accuracy of these facts on the ground, and know them to be true. My Hasbany friend, who is a sort of travelling merchant, sold the shrouds of the victims, and saw nine of them buried the next morning. I have often felt the extreme power of these winds to cool down the vital heat of the body, but never encountered anything like this. It reminds one of David's horrible tempests."[2]

As the storm clouds scurried down from the north they first obscured and then quenched the last gleams of the sunset. Soon large drops of rain began to fall. Fearful of taking shelter under a tree, Mary and Joseph hurried along the way to the town before the storm burst in its full fury. They reached the crest of the ridge and hastened down the track which the winter's rain and the feet of many travellers had churned into soft mud. Jolting, stumbling, slipping in the darkness, they squelched through the mud, but they did not fall, for the ass was sure-footed and Mary was supported by Joseph's strong arm. They were overtaken and passed by less encumbered travellers, all impatient for shelter. Drenched with the pelting rain, confused by the deafening thunder, bewildered by the forked lightning, shouted at and thrust aside by more active people, at length they managed to reach the end of the perilous slope and saw the wall of the town loom up before them. In the vault of the gateway they paused to recover breath and shake the rain from their garments. Other travellers were there who halted to look out at the battle of the elements, for now the storm had attained its full force and broke in an appalling downpour. The flying clouds were torn into jagged shapes by the serrated mountain ridges, the wind seemed to scream in its violence, the bitter cold wind from the snows of Hermon. The thunder bellowed and rumbled, not in short and separate peals, but in long, continuous rolls, while the flashes of lightning stabbed down at the earth and seemed to follow each other without interval. The black ravens croaked as they were tossed in the blast, the white owls cowered like little ghosts in the crevices of the walls, and the hungry dogs howled with fear as the lightning drove them back to their dens. The streams, already swollen by the winter rain, and now frightfully augmented by the inundation of the storm, poured down the wadies in furious torrents. No wonder that the Israelites saw in a storm a manifestation of the power of Jehovah and heard His voice in the hurricane (cf. Ps. 17: 10–17). Joseph lost no time in finding good quarters for the night. They dried their garments at a fire, partook of their frugal supper, and gladly reposed their weary limbs.

The rising sun awoke Mary and Joseph to another day, the last of their journey. When it was bright enough to distinguish between the colours blue and white in the clear, wind-swept sky, they said their morning prayers. Then they broke bread, saddled the ass, and set off on the final stage of ten miles to Jerusalem and five more to Bethlehem. As the cocks were sounding reveille, they came out into the wet fields where the donkeys brayed and the camels curled a supercilious lip at the wintry sun. It was cold, very cold, and Joseph was solicitous to wrap Mary well in her heavy mantle and shawl. On they went up and down the undulating track that wound through the rounded hills of Judea. The hillsides were intensely cultivated on the terrace system: rows of olive and fig trees rose one above the other, and famous vineyards were all about, now, of course, bare sticks in winter.

At length they reached the hill of Sapha, which Josephus interprets as Scopus, a place of observation. Here they got their first clear view of the Holy City, and they paused, as pilgrims did, to recite a gradual psalm. There it was, David's capital, newly strengthened and embellished by Herod, surrounded by its walls with their hundred towers, with the lofty façade of the

Temple, "the Mountain of the House," its gold and marble glittering in the pale beams of the sun. The rabbis proudly said: "The Universe is like to an eye: the white of the eye is the ocean surrounding the world; the black is the world itself; the pupil is Jerusalem; and the image in the pupil is the Temple."[3] After their pause of prayer and contemplation, Mary and Joseph descended the slope into the northern part of the Kidron Valley, and then ascended again to the level of the city, set on its high table-land. They passed through groves of olive trees and emerged among the market gardens that ran up almost to the walls of the city. There was a veritable maze of these gardens and orchards intersected by cross-walls and cactus hedges and trenches,[4] and full of pit-falls for the unwary in the shape of rock cisterns, into the open mouths of which the stranger might stumble. Cucumbers, melons, leeks, onions, and garlic were grown in these gardens as well as the lowly plants of mint, anise, and cummin which the Pharisees were so scrupulous to tithe (cf. Matt. 23:23). Figs, almonds, walnuts, carobs, pomegranates, mulberry, and lemon were grown for profit and for grateful shade in the long summer heats. Mary and Joseph were not fast travellers, and so they were overtaken and passed by strings of laden donkeys and camels hastening in to the city market.

Soon they arrived under the shadow of the mighty walls and saw the northern gate looming up before them. It was known as the Damascus Gate, for it was the starting point of the road to the great Syrian city, and also as the Fish Gate, probably because through its portals entered the fish consignments from the Lake of Tiberias. Mary and Joseph had no business in Jerusalem; their need was to reach Bethlehem before sunset, and they would travel more easily in the open than through the congested lanes and alleys of the city. So they turned to the right and skirted the lofty walls.

What were Mary's feelings as she passed by Jerusalem? It was her birth-place, and contained the house of her parents where she had passed the days of her infancy. There, too, was the well-known Temple, in the courts of which she had grown up. Indeed it was in the shelter of the Temple that she had spent most of her young life. It was not much more than a year since she had left Jerusalem for Nazareth, and in that short year so much had happened, her betrothal, the coming of the angel, her three months' visit to Elizabeth when she had passed Jerusalem going and coming, her return to Nazareth, and her wedding. Now she is at Jerusalem again, this time with her husband. A thousand years previously David, her ancestor, had made Jerusalem the capital, but now she would not tarry within its walls. She was going on to Bethlehem, the City of David, there to give birth to the Son of David, the Messias, the Consolation of Israel, for whose coming prophets, priests, and people had prayed.

They followed the path that meandered between the low, stone walls and cactus hedges which separated one man's property from another, treading carefully so as to avoid falling into the mouths of cisterns. The ground must have been honeycombed with these artificial receptacles for rain-water, for each proprietor liked to have his own cistern on his own land. The length of the long dry summer from May to September and the scarcity of springs made the conservation of rain-water a necessity. There is no river in Jerusalem. Hence from the earliest times many cisterns were dug in the limestone rock. Some were bottle-shaped to prevent evaporation, some were rectangular, like stone tanks, and some were built of masonry overground. They were to be found everywhere, by the waysides, in vineyards, and gardens and under the houses (cf. Jer. 2:13). Jeremias refers to the rock-hewn cisterns of Jerusalem, and it appears that each house had its own cistern for the collection of the precious water (cf. 4 Kings 18:31). "Stolen waters are sweeter," says Proverbs (9:17), but nevertheless each man is advised to "drink water out of thy own cistern" (Prov. 5:15). The fact that drinking water was liable to be stolen is an indication of its value and scarcity. In many places where no spring water was available, cisterns were necessary, not only for domestic use, but for irrigation and the watering of animals. It was in a wayside cistern which had gone dry that the first Joseph was confined by his jealous brethren (cf. Gen. 37:24), and the prophet Jeremias was imprisoned by being let down with ropes into a cistern in which the muddy deposit was still soft (cf. Jer. 38:6). Water was drawn up in a jar let down by a cord, or by a rope unwound by a hand-wheel over the larger cisterns. Sometimes the mouths of cisterns were closed by large stones (cf. Gen. 29:2), as the wells of the desert. But in proximity to a town where recourse to the cistern was more frequent, less clumsy coverings were provided.[5] Josephus relates that the mouths of wells and cisterns were covered with boards, and sometimes even surrounded by low palisades to prevent men or animals from falling into them.[6]

Mary and Joseph knew, of course, that during the recent rains the mouths of the cisterns had been opened, and that it was quite likely that some careless owners had neglected or forgotten to close them, thus leaving positive pit-falls for the feet of the unwary. They rounded the north-western angle of the city wall and proceeded on their way. On their left the great wall towered up into the sky; on their right was a low garden wall enclosing the property of a wealthy man known as Joseph of Arimathea, who afterwards became a member of the Sanhedrin. Their path wound along beside this garden until it was intersected by the main route from Jaffa, which entered the city by the Gate of Ephraim on their left. This road was usually thronged with people coming and going, and there were the usual crowds of people in the market place outside the gate, buying, selling, and gossiping, with the inevitable poor folk begging alms from the passers-by. Suddenly they heard the sound of a trumpet and, looking across, they saw that a Pharisee in his white robes had come forth from under the gateway and was about to distribute largesse. One servant blew the trumpet and another carried the money bag. Instantly there was a wild scramble of poor wretches toward this ostentatious alms-giver (cf. Matt. 6:2).

The spectacle was too common to detain Mary and Joseph, so they crossed the main road to Jaffa and continued on. On the other side of this road an isolated rock rose out of the ground. It was about fifteen feet in height and width. There was nothing remarkable about it except its shape, which fanciful people likened to a human head. So it was known as Golgotha, "the Place of the Skull." "And they came to the place that is called Golgotha, which is, the place of Calvary" (Matt. 27:33). St. John adds that it "was nigh to the city" (19:20). Calvary is the Latin translation of Golgotha. The rock is never described by the evangelists as a hill or a mount, nor do its small dimensions merit such a description. It was just one of the many rocks jutting out of the stony soil, but its proximity to a city gate and its position beside a main route made it suitable for the dreadful purpose to which it was later put by the Romans when they took over the government of Judea. In much later times the evil fame of this ugly rock caused its name to be magnified into Mount Calvary. Calvary is 140 feet south-east of the Holy Sepulchre and at present is 13 feet higher.

On the city side a kind of rough ascent led up to the top of the rock. The beginning of this ascent is only 30 paces from the Gate.[7] As Mary's eyes rested on the Rock of the Skull had she any presentiment of the future?

As Mary and Joseph moved along the wall, they rounded another angle of the massive rampart and saw the new palace of Herod with its three tremendous towers out-topping the high wall. There was "the tower Hippicus, and close to it two others, all built by King Herod into the old wall, and for magnitude, beauty, and strength, without their equal in the world. For, apart from his innate magnanimity and his pride in the city, the king sought, in the super-excellence of these works, to gratify his private feelings, dedicating them to the memory of the three persons to whom he was most fondly attached, and after whom he named these towers — brother, friend, and wife [that is, Phasael, Hippicus, and Mariamne]. They seemed far larger owing to their site. For the old wall in which they stood was itself built into a lofty hill, and above the hill rose as it were a crest thirty cubits higher still; on this the towers stood and thus gained immensely in elevation."[8] Mary and Joseph saw the portal at the Gate Genaath, or the Garden Gate, in the old wall below the lofty towers. It was facing west, and from it the road ran south to Bethlehem. Leaving Jerusalem behind them, Mary and Joseph took this road and began the last lap of their journey.

CHAPTER 10

On the Road to Bethlehem

OUR Christmas cards show snow on the ground at Bethlehem, and our carols sing of a white Christmas. But, when we recollect that Palestine is a sub-tropical country, we begin to doubt the snow. Yet we are unwilling to discard our belief that the first Christmas was a snowy one, and so we inquire if snow does really fall in Palestine, and we are pleased to learn that it does. All the year round snow lies deep in the ravines of Lebanon, and Hermon's great shoulder is covered with perpetual snow. But these are mountains: does snow ever fall in the low land? Jerusalem and Bethlehem are situated in mountainous country: Jerusalem lies at levels between 2300 and 2500 feet above the Mediterranean, and Bethlehem is 2550 feet above sea-level. In fact, a temperature of 25 degrees Fahrenheit has been recorded in Jerusalem, which is seven degrees below the freezing point.[1] Snow actually does fall in Jerusalem and Bethlehem, but rarely lies for long on the ground.

The climate cannot have changed very much since New Testament times, and there are two references to falls of snow in the historical books of the Bible, besides numerous references in the other books. Benaias the priest, one of David's champion fighting men, "went down and killed a lion in the midst of a pit in the time of snow" (1 Par. 11:22; 2 Kings 23:20). This pit was probably an unused cistern. "From this we learn several things: that lions abounded in the land in the time of David; that they retreated into pits; and, lastly, that they had snowy days even in Palestine."² Another verse of the Bible records a fall of snow heavy enough to hold up the advance of an army. "And Tryphon made ready all his horsemen to come that night: but there fell a very great snow, and he came not into the country of Galaad" (1 Mach. 13:22). Jericho is only seventeen miles from Jerusalem, but it is situated down in the torrid trench of the Jordan Valley where the Dead Sea is 1292 feet below the level of the Mediterranean and where the snow never falls. Josephus has this to say of Jericho: "Moreover, the climate is so mild that the inhabitants wear linen when snow is falling throughout the rest of Judea."³ So in his days snow did fall in Judea, and he was a native of Jerusalem and a contemporary of St. John the Apostle.

In modern times, when G. K. Chesterton visited Jerusalem in 1919, he recorded that "it snowed day and night until that eastern city was sealed up like a village in Norway or Northern Scotland. It rose in the streets till men might almost have been drowned in it like a sea of solid foam."⁴ A chaplain of the R.A.F. attended midnight Mass in the Basilica of Bethlehem, and when he came out, he was thrilled to see snow lying on the ground: "In the morning snow fell in Bethlehem."⁵ In January, 1950, snow was so heavy and so continuous that the branches of many trees were broken by its weight, and the Red Cross workers had to shovel away the snow in order to penetrate to the camps of the Arab refugees. So it is quite possible that a fall of snow added to the discomfort of Mary and Joseph in Bethlehem, and that the first Christmas was a white one.

Mary and Joseph passed close to the western wall of Jerusalem and descended into the Valley of Hinnom. To the left of the road to Bethlehem was a large pool known as the Dragon's Fountain or the Dragon's Well. There is no true spring hereabouts, and the Pool was really neither a fountain nor a well but a reservoir formed by throwing two dykes across the valley.

It was fed by rain-water and also probably by the overflow of the aqueduct from Solomon's Pools beyond Bethlehem. Its dimensions have been given as 555 feet from north to south and 220 feet from east to west. The depth at the northern end was some 36 feet, increasing to 42 feet at the southern or lower end.[6] This is probably the place referred to by Josephus as the Serpent's Pool,[7] for "dragon" and "serpent" seem to be synonymous in Hebrew. The pool was now full after the winter rains. Beyond it rose the Hill of Sion crowned by the wall enclosing the Upper City. To their right lay the open hill country of Judea. Mary, as her gaze swept across the landscape, must have thought of Ain Karim, for it was in this hill country, in the home of Zachary and Elizabeth, that she had recently spent three happy months.

The road sloped steeply into the Valley of Hinnom or Gehenna, and the holy couple left behind and above them the south-western corner of Mount Sion with the Dung Gate leading to the unsavoury valley. Here in former days degenerate kings had erected altars to Moloch, the grisly god of the Ammonites, the "fire-King" to whom innocent children were sacrificed. Eventually the good King Josiah overturned the abominable idol and led his people back to the worship of the true God. But the place was accurst, and "Gehenna" became a synonym for "hell." The deep, narrow glen became the city dump into which vile refuse was cast: dead bodies of criminals, carcasses of animals, bones, broken pots, rubbish, and filth of all kinds. All that was combustible was burnt, the rest was left to putrefy. Here the smoke of continuous fires rose into the air, for here, indeed, the "worm dieth not, and the fire is not extinguished" (Mark 9:45). It was popularly believed that the mouth of hell was situated here. "There are two palm trees in the Valley of Hinnom, between which a smoke ariseth; and this is the door of Gehenna."[8]

As Mary and Joseph plodded upwards they left behind them the smoke and smells of the horrible valley. Soon they reached the level ground, the Plain of Rephaim, where their ancestor David had fought two battles against the Philistines. On the right hand side of the track they saw a solitary terebinth or turpentine tree rise from the field to a height of twenty feet. It had a thick, gnarled trunk, numerous long branches, and slender twigs, now bare of their summer leaves and berries.[9] They passed the terebinth, but legend relates that they halted there with the Child on their return from Bethlehem. Farther on they reached a wayside well on the left, and here, it is said, they paused a while to rest. Mary's time was very near at hand, and some rest would seem to be necessary. Joseph made her as comfortable as he could on the lee side of the wall of the well, and they probably had some refreshment. The food and a cup of wine warmed Mary and she felt able to continue. But Joseph would not hurry her, for they had only about four miles to go, and, though it may have been snowing, there would still be daylight for some hours yet. So, from their sheltered nook by the well they looked out upon the passers-by.

Because of the cold and the snow, however, Joseph would not linger too long by the well. Reverently he helped Mary mount, and they proceeded on their way. In ten minutes they reached a rocky hill from which both Jerusalem and Bethlehem were visible. A late tradition of the Greek Church has it that this was the spot where the Prophet Elias rested on his flight from the vengeance of Queen Jezabel, and so they erected a convent here and called it Mar Elias.

But there was no convent on the hill when Joseph halted there to view Bethlehem. They paused a while on the ridge, a little group silhouetted against the leaden sky, Mary seated on the donkey, Joseph standing beside her, propping her up so that she might have a better view, the cold wind blowing the fringes of their mantles, and the snow flakes whirling around them. Behind them lay Jerusalem, the stony city on its hill of stone. But in front of them was Bethlehem, "the House of Bread," in its fertile fields. As Mary's eyes rested on the little town, her heart must have skipped a beat and her breath must have come faster, for it was the place appointed by God to be the birthplace of her Son. "If the general aspect of Jerusalem and the memories which this city recalls awakens in the soul a grave and solemn feeling, full of greatness but at the same time full of sadness, the pilgrim experiences different emotions at the sight of Bethlehem. I do not know what serene and sweet joy hovers over this gracious village, which instead of having, like the Holy City, to weep over the Death and over the Tomb of God, encloses and shows again with a religious gladness the place of His Birth and the site of His cradle. It is indeed the homeland of Him for whom the world of old had sighed so long and who should beget a new life for the modern world. Here there is an everlasting halo of joy in Christian eyes which seems to encompass the face of this little town, and I would sincerely pity those who tread for the first time the soil of Bethlehem and who do not feel from the bottom of the heart one of these ineffable satisfactions which make the whole soul thrill, because they come, not from the earth, but from Heaven."[10] Mary's feelings were too deep for words as she looked at Bethlehem. The silence was rudely broken by the click of hooves on the pebbles as the donkey shivered and moved downhill, for the poor beast was cold and impatient for stabling and rest.

Over to their left they had a clear view of a conical hill which aroused different emotions. Forty-two years previously Herod had defeated the partisans of Antigonus, his rival for the crown, and to celebrate the victory he built a town at the foot of this hill which he named Herodia, and on the summit a castle which he named Herodium, which he intended to be the mausoleum of his family. The place "was strong by nature, and fit for such a building. It is a sort of moderate hill, raised to a farther height by the hand of man, till it was the shape of a woman's breast. It is encompassed by circular towers, and hath a straight ascent up to it, which ascent is composed of polished stones, in number two hundred. Within are royal and very rich apartments, of structure that provided both for security and for beauty."[11] Thus wrote Josephus, who must have known the place well. The Herodium, accordingly, was palace, citadel, and mausoleum. Mary and Joseph gazed at this glittering new castle of the usurper dominating the city of David, their royal ancestor, the beloved of God and the darling of the people. After the fall of Jerusalem in A.D. 70, the Herodium became a bandit's lair and was destroyed by the Romans. At the present day not a trace remains of the tomb of Herod.

When they had descended from the ridge they saw Jerusalem no more. In a few minutes they reached the tomb of Rachel on the left of the way. Bethlehem is mentioned for the first time in Genesis, the first book of the Bible, under two names, Bethlehem and Ephrata. Both names are interesting. Ephrata means "fertile," and Bethlehem, "the house of bread," so both names testify to the good land of the place. St. Jerome apostrophises it thus: "Hail, Bethlehem, house of bread, wherein was born that Bread which came down from heaven! Hail, Ephrata, land of fruitfulness and fertility, whose fruit is the Lord Himself!"[12]

It was now about a thousand years since David was born in Bethlehem, and even then the town was old, for Jacob and his clan had halted there almost a thousand years before the birth of David. It was there that the Patriarch had suffered the greatest sorrow of his life, the death of his beloved Rachel. "He came in the springtime to the land which leadeth to Ephrata; wherein when Rachel was in travail, by reason of her hard labour she began to be in danger, and the midwife said to her: Fear not, for thou shalt have this son also. And when her soul was departing for pain, and death was now at hand, she called the name of her son Benoni, that is, The son of my pain: but his father called him Benjamin, that is, The son of the right hand. So Rachel died, and was buried in the highway that leadeth to Ephrata, this is Bethlehem. And Jacob erected a pillar over her sepulchre: this is the pillar of Rachel's monument, to this day. Departing thence, he pitched his tent beyond the Flock tower"

(Gen. 35:16–21). Rachel's is the first death from childbirth mentioned in the Bible, and her pillar is its first recorded example of a sepulchral monument. It was a landmark in the time of David, for to it Saul was directed (cf. 1 Kings 10:2). The monument erected by Jacob has been replaced time and again down the centuries. It had become a pyramid before the Crusades. The Crusaders surrounded it with arches and put a cupola over all. The Moslems built up the arches and made the little building resemble a Moslem shrine. The pyramid has disappeared and is replaced by a cenotaph. In 1841 the Anglo-Jewish millionaire Montefiore obtained the key of the building for the Jews, the first shrine which they acquired in Palestine.[13] They have lost it in the recent fighting and it has reverted to the Moslems. At present it is dirty outside and dingy within. But it is one of the best authenticated sites in the Holy Land. Mary saw the Tomb of Rachel as she passed by; perhaps in the circumstances it suggested painful thoughts to her. Mary and Joseph were descended from Jacob, but not from Rachel. Their lineage went back to Juda, who was the son of Jacob by his first wife Lia, the elder sister of Rachel.

Beyond the tomb the way divided. The right fork went to Hebron, about twelve miles farther on; the left to Bethlehem, less than a mile away. Across the fields to their left the holy couple saw the famous cistern from which David longed to drink. At the time David was fleeing from Saul and hiding in the cave of Adullam (cf. 2 Kings 23:14). At last they neared the end of their journey, for Bethlehem lay before them on its ridge, its white houses surrounded by the grey wall bright under the leaden sky. From the town the ground fell away on all sides in terraced slopes. These terraces, as they swept in graceful curves round the ridge, gave the place the aspect of an amphitheatre, a picturesque scene which the approaching traveller does not easily forget. The surrounding hills, though they appear bare, nevertheless are the grazing pastures of flocks of sheep and herds of goats. They saw the sheep following the shepherds to the stone pens for the night, and they heard the piping of the shepherd's flutes and the tinkling of the little bells on the necks of the bell-wethers. The terraced slopes between the fields and the town were intensely cultivated. They passed through the bare groves of olive, fig, vine, pomegranate, peach, and almond, now, of course, without a bloom showing, except perhaps the pink of the almond, the first waker of the year. The valleys beyond the town and the fields to the east and to the sunny south were sown with wheat and barley and were so productive that they gave the place its name, "the house of bread." They remembered the story of Ruth, the Moabite, the charming woman who became the mother of David's grandfather, and of how in her widowed youth she gleaned the portion of the poor in these very fields:

> *. . . the sad heart of Ruth, when, sick for home,*
> *She stood in tears amid the alien corn.*

But as Mary and Joseph plodded up the rise to the town, they were dismayed to see the open space before the gate occupied by a noisy multitude of people.

CHAPTER 11

No Room in the Inn

WHY was there no room in Bethlehem for Mary and Joseph? The learned commentators assign three probable causes: the number of strangers gathered for the census, the alleged poverty of Mary and Joseph, and the lateness of their arrival. Lagrange says: "Great numbers of people must have been brought to the registration office which had been established there."[1] A Lapide maintains that all the places in the inn were already occupied by the crowd of richer people brought by the census and that here there was only one inn, as St. Luke indicates by his use of the definite article.[2] Maldonatus contends that the multitude of the kindred of David crowding into the town was the principal cause and that poor Mary and Joseph could not compete with the wealthier visitors.[3] Lebreton says: "Doubtless the enrollment had brought a great concourse of strangers to Bethlehem and the humble travellers from Galilee came too late and were too poor to find a place."[4] Fillion wrote: "Other Israelites, whose families belonged originally to the City of David, had also been summoned by the edict of Augustus and they had arrived before the parents of Jesus. These latter found not only the private houses, but also the town's single khan or caravansary filled."[5] Fouard says: "The concourse of strangers in those busy days of registration, the poverty of these late comers, the very condition of Mary, promised to the humble pair a cold welcome."[6]

If there were only one inn, as seems probable enough, it must
have been a large one, for Bethlehem was on the direct route to
Egypt, and merchant caravans need ample space for their strings
of camels, bales of goods, and numerous attendants when they
halt for the night. Doubtless, some people did come to Bethlehem for registration, but who were they? The descendants of
David, and also natives of the place who had moved their habitation elsewhere. This latter class could not have formed a large
proportion of the population, for the peasants of the period were
rooted in the soil, and no man desired to leave the shadow of his
own vine and fig-tree. Besides, the primitive highways, the lack
of quick transport, the perils of the way, the fear of the unknown,
and religious difficulties were all reasons for keeping the peasant
at home and making him reluctant to undertake long journeys.
The Bethlehemites were mainly an agricultural people, and their
fruit trees, crops, vineyards, cattle, and sheep needed their personal attention all year round. No man in those days travelled
for pleasure. The only long journey which the peasant of Palestine was willing to undertake was the pilgrimage to the Temple.
Of course, economic stress, then as now, would compel superfluous sons to leave the home and seek their fortune elsewhere.
These would be expected to return for the census. Their numbers
could not have been so large as to tax the accommodation of the
town to the limit, and naturally these people would seek and
obtain shelter with their relatives.

It is impossible at this distant date to fix the population of
Bethlehem at the first Christmas. One learned author estimates
it to have been little more than one thousand souls, mostly shepherds and poor peasants.[7] Another's estimate is two thousand
people.[8] It is hard to discover the evidence for these figures.
Josephus declares that none of the towns and villages of Galilee
contained less than fifteen thousand inhabitants.[9] If his figures
be correct, and, after all, he was in a position to know, then it
is likely that the towns of Judea, of which Bethlehem was one,
were not less populous. Even today Bethlehem has seven

thousand five hundred inhabitants, and the country was more prosperous and more thickly populated in New Testament times.

How many descendants of David were assembled in Bethlehem for the census? David had been dead for about a thousand years, but the successors of his line had been reigning monarchs for about four hundred years afterwards. The genealogies in the Gospels show the direct male line from David down to Joseph, so he was probably the head of the House of David in his own time. The House and Family of David could not have numbered many adult male members in his time. In the United Kingdom the Royal Family is the term given to the sovereign and members of his family, including uncles, aunts, and cousins. The line goes back nearly nine hundred years, to the coronation of the founder, William the Conqueror, in 1066. At the present day the British Royal Family does not number a score of adult persons. Herod the Great was the first king of his line, and at his death the House of Herod did not consist of more than a score of adult persons. Their names can be counted in any genealogical list of his family. At the date of the Nativity the House of David probably numbered less adults. They could not have been so numerous as to occupy all available space in all the houses as well as the inn of Bethlehem. In the next generation the Emperor Domitian (A.D. 81–96) sought them out with all the resources of the empire at his disposal, and there were found living only two adult male members of the House of David.[10]

It is unlikely that the combined members of the House of David and the returned exiles of Bethlehem for the census could have filled the town to its utmost capacity. Can any other reason be assigned for the over-crowding? The simultaneous arrival of several large caravans would fill the inn. There must have been instances where the arrival of a caravan from the great mart of Damascus in the north en route to Egypt coincided with the coming of another from Alexandria, the second city of the empire. Another possible explanation would be that Mary and Joseph came on one of the fair days of Bethlehem, when the people from many miles around would pour into the market. In Jerusalem "the original market days were Monday and Tuesday, afterwards Friday. Besides, every caravansary, or khan, was a sort of mart, where goods were unloaded, and especially cattle set out for sale, and purchases made."[11] The incidence of a fair day would be a simple and natural explanation for the over-crowding of the town and the inn. Doctor Thomson gives an animated description of one of the weekly fairs held at Khan et Tejjar, "The Inn of the Merchants." When he wrote about a hundred years ago, fairs were much the same as they had been from time immemorial:

"On Monday of each week a great fair is held at the khans, when, for a few hours, the scene is very lively and picturesque. These gatherings afford an excellent opportunity to observe Syrian manners, customs, and costumes, and to become acquainted with the character and quality of Syrian productions. Thousands of people assemble from all parts of the country, either to sell, trade, or purchase. Cotton is brought in bales from Nablus; barley, and wheat, and sesamun, and Indian corn from the Huleh, the Hauran, and Esdraelon. From Gilead and Bashan, and the surrounding districts, come horses and donkeys, cattle and flocks, with cheese, leben, semen, honey, and similar articles. Then there are miscellaneous matters, such as chickens and eggs, figs, raisins, apples, melons, grapes, and all sorts of fruits and vegetables in their season. The pedlars open their packages of tempting fabrics; the jeweller is there with his trinkets; the tailor with his ready-made garments; the shoemaker with his stock, from rough, hairy sandals to yellow and red morocco boots; the farrier is there with his tools, nails and flat iron shoes, and drives a prosperous business for a few hours; and so does the saddler, with his coarse sacks and gaily-trimmed cloths. And thus it is with all the arts and occupations known to this people.

"The noise is incessant, and at a distance sounds like that 'of many waters.' Every man is crying his wares at the top of his voice, chickens cackle and squall, donkeys bray and fight, and the dogs bark. Every living thing adds somewhat to the many-toned and prodigious uproar. It is now a miscellaneous comedy in full operation, where every actor does his best, and is supremely gratified with his own performance.

"The people find many reasons for sustaining these antiquated and very curious gatherings. Every man, woman, and child has inherited a strong desire for trading, and, of course, all classes meet at this grand bourse to talk over the state of the markets, from the price of a cucumber to that of cotton, or of a five-thousand dollar horse from the Hauran. Again, every Arab is a politician, and groups gather around the outskirts of the crowd to discuss the doings of the 'allied powers,' the last firman from the sultan, or the new tax demanded by their own petty emeer. Descending to more ordinary matters, these fairs are great places for gossip and scandal. Friends meet friends, and exchange the news of weddings, births, and deaths, and all the multifarious incidents and accidents between these grand extremes of human life. In a word, these fairs supply the places of many of the appliances of more civilized society. They are the daily news-paper, for there is one for every day within a circuit of forty miles. They are the exchange, and the forwarding office, and the political caucus, and the family gathering, and the grand festa and gala days; and underlying the whole is the ever-present idea and aim of making money."[12]

Some of the commentators imply that there was no room in the inn for Mary and Joseph because they were too poor to pay for the necessary accommodation. Elsewhere we have adduced evidence to show that they were not so poor at all.[13] Furthermore, the inn was free. Most of these Eastern Khans are, like the mosques, charitable foundations supported by the generosity of the descendants of the donor. A man of trust, paid from funds set apart for that purpose, receives the caravans, opens the doors every morning and closes them every evening. If travellers do not require any personal services from him, they need not give him any money whatever, no matter how long they stay. The keeper is content to supplement his wages by a modest profit on the straw, fire-wood, and sour milk which he sells to the travellers.[14] The two denarii disbursed by the Good Samaritan to the inn-keeper were remuneration for his personal attendance on the wounded man, not payment for lodging, which was free to all (cf. Luke 10:35). Surely Joseph, a skilled artisan in a booming trade, was not so poor as to be able to afford a trifle for clean straw and a morsel of firewood.

The rule of the khan was first come first served. The earliest arrivals naturally occupied the best places in the alcoves on the *leewan* or platform raised above the level of the courtyard. Some of the commentators imply that Mary and Joseph arrived so late as to find the place full. Joseph, the man chosen by almighty God to be the husband of His Mother, was no laggard. For such an event as the Nativity he would make sure that Mary arrived in good time in Bethlehem. Besides, the last stage of the journey was not so long. From Beeroth to Jerusalem is only ten miles and from there to Bethlehem not more than six miles. Mary was not a fast traveller, but surely they could do sixteen miles in less than the eight hours of daylight of a winter's day and arrive in Bethlehem long before dark.

That there was an inn in Bethlehem is explicitly stated by the evangelist. Is anything known of its history? It was a charitable foundation on land originally donated by David him-self. When the revolt of Absalom forced his father to take refuge beyond the Jordan, David and his weary followers were hospi-tably received by Berzellai, an aged sheik of Galaad. The King never forgot this kindness shown to him in adversity, and when he returned triumphant to Jerusalem, he begged his host to accompany him. But Berzellai pleaded his great age, and sent his son Chimham instead to partake in the festivals of the restor-ation. When David was dying, he commended the family of Berzellai to his successor Solomon. "But shew kindness to the sons of Berzellai the Galaadite, and let them eat at thy table: for they met me when I fled from the face of Absalom thy

brother" (3 kings 2:7). From the reference to "and sat as
sojourners in Chamaan [Chimham], which is near Bethlehem"
(Jer. 41:17), it has been inferred that David had rewarded
Chimham by a grant from his patrimonial acres at Bethlehem.
The Hebrew word rendered by "habitation" is *Geruth,* which
signifies an inn or khan.[15] Apparently Chimham built this to
shelter his flocks and herds — and their attendants — on their
way to the market of Jerusalem from beyond the Jordan.

When Mary and Joseph drew nigh to the walls of Bethlehem,
they were disconcerted to see the multitude outside the gate and
to hear the shouts of men, the lowing of cattle, the braying of
donkeys, and the barking of dogs. Mary's heart must have sunk
within her as she realised that the presence of this multitude
diminished their chances of finding quarters for the night. And
she had been looking forward to the end of the journey, to a
clean bed, hot water, a warm fire, and, above all, privacy for the
birth of the Messias. The sight of that noisy multitude must
have brought tears to the eyes of the gentle girl-mother and
anguish to the heart of her faithful guardian. The apocryphal
gospel, known as the *Protoevangelium,* supplies this touching
detail. "And when Joseph looked back, he saw the face of Mary,
that it was sorrowful, as of one in pain; but when he looked
back again, she smiled. And when they were come to Bethlehem, there was no room for them in the inn, because of the
great concourse of people. And Mary said to Joseph: 'Take me
down, for I suffer.'" It would be typical of Mary to spare the
feelings of Joseph by hiding her own. How many times on the
way had he looked anxiously at her, and how many times had
she smiled bravely back to reassure him. And now this crushing
disappointment! Before Mary dismounted, Joseph carefully led
the ass across the market place, stepping warily through the
muck churned up by the feet of men and animals, threading
his way between the groups of gossiping friends and excited
bargainers, dodging the lines of couchant camels and penned
sheep, until they reached the gateway. Then Mary dismounted,

and they wormed their way through the chattering groups that encumbered the entrance.

If the market place without had been congested, the town within was full. The visitors filled the houses: they occupied the flat roofs and invaded the inner chambers. There were people squatting in corners of the courtyards and sitting under the arches of the narrow streets, as the Levite and his wife had done in Gabaa, "for no man would receive them to lodge" (Judges 19:15). Even nowadays the Palestinian peasant, if pressed, can resign himself to the most primitive accommodation; can sleep in the dust under a wall. The crooked streets and lanes were blocked by great hulking camels, past which the patient donkey had to squeeze its way. The townsmen, driving in their milch cows for the night, were furious with the press of strangers that obstructed traffic. The shouting of angry men and the lowing of impatient cows increased the discordant din. Joseph was appalled at the congestion, but he took courage when he remembered that he was a "Son of David" and that Bethlehem was the headquarters of his clan. He would make for the house of a kinsman. The bond of blood, so sacred in the East, would surely open a door for him. Hopefully he pushed forward, ever ready to interpose his body when either man or beast threatened to press too closely on the slight veiled figure walking behind him or to thrust her roughly against the wall. Slowly, patiently, step by step they advanced until they reached the house of their kinsman. The winter evening was cold, but when they halted at the door, Joseph was wiping sweat from his brow.

There is a striking picture by M. Tissot of the scene at the foot of the flight of steps leading up from the street to the upper room of their relative's house. There are such exterior staircases to be seen in Bethlehem at the present day. The tired donkey wearily droops its head towards the cobblestones, and Mary has resumed her seat, wrapped in her dark blue mantle. Her white shawl envelops her head and shoulders and, though she holds its corner towards her face, it can be seen that she is crying softly. Joseph, wallet on hip, arm aloft, is calling up the steps. In the opposite house the heads of two curious women are projecting from the lattice above their closed door. A man carrying a bundle is climbing up the steps of the next house, and a woman bearing a child on her back is hurrying home. From under the arch, or rather the tunnel beneath the upper stories, a man with a camel is bearing down on the little group. The woman of the house appears on the top of the staircase. In response to Joseph's urgent calling and beckoning, she shakes her head, and waves her arms at them to go away. Her attitude is unmistakable and expresses a definite refusal. Probably her house is really full; probably nearer relatives have already claimed her hospitality; perhaps she would have taken in Mary and Joseph if she could. Anyhow, she plainly indicates that she has no room for them.[16]

So they had to try elsewhere. Picture them going from house to house through the packed streets, dismayed by the multitude, bewildered by the uproar. But every door was closed in their faces and no man would receive them to lodge. "No room, no room," was the invariable reply to Joseph's patient pleading. The traditional hospitality of the East was great, but on that night it was overtaxed. How the inhabitants must have resented the multitude of strangers clamoring at their doors! Some of the women must have perceived that Mary was in imminent need of shelter, but none of these harassed housewives desired to add the confinement of a strange woman to their already over-burdened household. Mary's condition in ordinary times would doubtless have won her sympathetic consideration, but it must have militated against her reception on that particular night. Still, if one woman had contrived to make room for them that night, her house would have been made glorious for all time as the birthplace of the Saviour. But it was not to be. What must have been the feelings of Joseph when at last he realised that every door was barred to them? He looked again at Mary, who sat patiently on the donkey, drooping with fatigue. He must find shelter somewhere and at once, for her need was imperative. Since no house would admit them, they would go to the bare walls of the inn. Joseph gripped the bridle of the donkey, set his shoulders squarely, and plunged once more into the maelstrom. His body forged through the milling multitude, like the prow of a ship through heavy waves, thrusting aside all that impeded his course.

The keeper of the khan was posted at the gate and he barred further entry. Mary lifted her veil and turned her liquid eyes upon him beseechingly, while Joseph begged for a place on the *leewan* raised above the dirt and droppings of the yard, for a nook among the bales of the merchants, for any spot at all. But the keeper glanced at Mary and shook his head. He was not going to add a confinement to his other responsibilities on that busy night. The place was crowded anyhow, so he had no hesitation in saying significantly that there was no room — for them — in the inn. But when Mary looked through the gateway and heard the tumult within, she was frightened by the publicity of the place. She needed privacy quite as much as shelter and there was no possible privacy there. "The inn of those days was much like a modern caravansary: a square area surrounded by high walls through which a single door gave entrance. There travelers and beasts of burden were sure to find water and shelter for the night. Animals spent the night in the open central courtyard, while their owners retired to a sort of platform on one or more sides of the quadrangle. Besides the large common room there were often small alcoves for rent at moderate prices. This was where Mary and Joseph had hoped to find the privacy which they desired; but all the alcoves were occupied and the common room promised all the inconveniences of private houses, and more. Thus, there was no room *for them* at the inn."[17]

Mary recoiled from the scene in the khan. Indeed it was appalling in its noise and squalor. No woman with sensitive sensibilities would choose such a public place for her confinement. Any quiet quarters, provided they were private, were better than this place of prying eyes, chattering tongues, and inescapable publicity. So she beckoned to Joseph to come away. His eyes mutely asked—whither? She did not know, but God would provide. The pity of it! When they turned dejectedly away, there must have been bitter tears of anxiety, of disappointment, of uncertainty in the eyes of the youthful Mother. How helpless Joseph must have felt!

There was no room in the town, no room in the inn. There was no room in the city of David for the descendants of David; no room for Joseph, the representative on earth of God the Father, no room for Mary, the Virgin-Mother of the Son; there was no room for the Son of David Himself: "He came unto his own, and his own received him not" (John 1:11). They were turned away into the night, the bitter cold of a winter night in Judea. When tens of thousands of pilgrims came up to Jerusalem for the great feasts, it was the boast of the rabbis that there was room for all. "No man said to his neighbour: This place is too strait for me, that I may lodge in Jerusalem."[18] Bethlehem could never have been congested to such an extent, even for the census. Doubtless some place could have been found for them. The evangelist does not say that there was no room in the inn, but that there was no room for them in the inn, a significant difference. Evidently they were not wanted. Must Mary then await her hour in the open field at night, and in the snow? Was there no other prospect for the Mother of God? She looked at Joseph, her husband, her guardian, her best friend. After such rebuffs a lesser man would have despaired, would have bowed to the seeming inevitable, the impossibility of finding a lodging in Bethlehem. But Joseph was not to be daunted. He had been chosen by God Himself to be the foster-father of His Son, and he proved himself worthy of his vocation in this emergency. He found the stable. But what a shame that Mary, the lily of Israel, had to go to a stable to give birth to her Child!

CHAPTER 12

The Cave of Bethlehem

ST. LUKE states in his Gospel that Mary laid her newly-born Son "in a manger; because there was no room for them in the inn." A manger implies that the shelter found by Joseph was some kind of stable. Where did Joseph find this stable? In what part of Bethlehem was it situated? This stable is popularly supposed to have been in a cave situated in the open fields outside the walls of the town. On the contrary, however, it is almost certain that the stable formed part of the premises of the inn. "The manger was not in the inn, but probably belonged to it."[1] It was really as much an adjunct of the inn as underground cellars are of a modern hotel. "One finds still, and we have seen at Khan Djoub-Yousef, the true ancient caravanserai, with its arrangements very well understandable. The principal part is constituted by a large court surrounded by walls against which leans a covered gallery. As the Khan usually had its back to a hill, a number of refuges are there dug in the rock, where when nights are cold, the flocks are sheltered instead of stationing them under the peristyle or even in the open air in the middle of the court."[2] The traveller leads his donkey or camel, the shepherd his sheep, and the herdsman drives his cattle across the floor of the open court and then down a passage to these underground caves. When the gate of the inn is closed, the watchman takes up his station, and all is secure for the night.[3]

The keeper had refused them admission to the inn itself, but he allowed them to take shelter in one of the stables. Down there they could give him no trouble, for it is difficult to imagine what personal services could be expected of him in the circumstances. A gratuity from Joseph may have helped to gain them admission. Then the keeper may have been a humane man with a wife and children of his own. However, the fact is certain that they were permitted to go to the stable. With feelings of inexpressible relief they saw the keeper stand aside and allow them to enter the gate. Barely glancing at the crowded alcoves around, they picked their way across the littered floor, through the bales of merchandise. Under the archway in the back wall of the khan a flight of steps led down to an underground passage. By this time the short winter daylight was fading, and it was quite dark below. They paused at the top of the steps until Mary unpacked their lamp and filled it with oil. Joseph had no trouble in obtaining a light at the cooking fire in the nearest alcove. He put the lamp in her hand and she led the way down the slippery, unclean steps, and followed her with the donkey. When they reached the passage below, they moved along, seeking for an unoccupied stable. The caves must have been fairly full on that cold, winter night. They saw couchant camels chewing the cud, donkeys tethered to the mangers, and sheep and cattle from beyond the Jordan and the Negeb. No owner would expose his beasts to the weather in the unroofed courtyard above. Mary went slowly along past the mouth of each cave, lamp in hand.

They were fortunate enough to find one stable untenanted save by a solitary ox. They stepped in, Mary holding the lamp high above her head, and looked about. What did they see by its light? Just a rude cave, for it was little more. Its dimensions were forty feet long from east to west, sixteen feet in width, and ten feet high. There was neither window nor door, of course, it being ventilated from the passage outside. There was no furniture except the manger, and the floor was far from clean. Though the rock walls were cold they were dry, and there was a stone roof overhead. But in Mary's eyes the stable had a supreme advantage which compensated for its discomforts. It afforded a privacy unobtainable in the human habitations above, and the holy couple sought privacy rather than a place to sleep.

The evangelist does not state that the Saviour was born in a cave. His mention of the manger naturally indicates a stable of some sort, but he does not use the word "cave." How, then, do we know that the Saviour was born in this cave? The tradition of the first and second centuries has supplemented the gospel narrative on this point, telling us that the manger was in a cave, a fact of inestimable interest. St. Justin Martyr wrote down the tradition as he heard it, and he was a native of Palestine. He was born at Neapolis, the ancient Sichem, within forty miles of Bethlehem, early in the second century, and was thus a member of the generation that succeeded the Apostles. He is a witness to the belief of the early Christians who lived at Bethlehem itself. He wrote: "Since Joseph could not find any lodging in the village, he took up his quarters in a certain cave near the village; and it was while they were there that Mary gave birth to the Christ and laid Him in a manger."[4] In the next century the erudite Origen founded a school of Christian studies in Caesarea, and visited the Holy Places. He states that everyone knew the cave in which the Lord was born. He wrote: "With respect to the birth of Jesus in Bethlehem, if anyone desires, after the prophecy of Micah and after the history recorded in the Gospels by the disciples of Jesus, to have additional evidence from other sources, let him know that, in conformity with the narrative in the Gospel regarding His birth, there is shown at Bethlehem the cave where He was born, and the manger in the cave where He was wrapped in swaddling clothes. And this sight is greatly talked of in surrounding places, even among the enemies of the faith, it being said that in this cave was born that Jesus who is worshipped and reverenced by the Christians."[5]

Few of the holy places of Palestine have in their favour such an ancient and authentic tradition as the Cave of Bethlehem. In A.D. 132 the Emperor Hadrian attempted to desecrate the holy places by building over them shrines to the pagan gods. Fortunately this action served the useful purpose of marking them out until the cessation of the persecutions and the liberation of the Church by the first Christian Emperor, Constantine the Great, in the year A.D. 313. St. Jerome, the greatest Scriptural scholar of all, lived in Bethlehem for thirty-four years, from 386 to 420. He wrote: "From the time of Hadrian to the reign of Constantine, a period of about one hundred and eighty years, the spot which had witnessed the Resurrection was occupied by a figure of Jupiter; while on the rock where the Cross had stood, a marble statue of Venus was set up by the heathen and became an object of worship. The original persecutors, indeed, supposed that by polluting our holy places they would deprive us of our faith in the Passion and in the Resurrection. Even my own Bethlehem, as it now is, that most venerable spot in the whole world of which the psalmist sings, 'the truth hath sprung out of the earth,' was overshadowed by a grove of Tammuz, that is, of Adonis; and in the very cave where the Infant Christ had uttered His earliest cry, lamentation was made for the paramour of Venus."⁶

But in the year 330, Helena Augusta, "the pious mother of a pious Emperor," as she is styled by the historian Eusebius, indignantly pulled down the temple of Adonis, and erected in its place the Church of the Nativity. Eusebius, the historian, who was a personal friend of Constantine, wrote of St. Helena: "For without delay, she dedicated two churches to the God whom she adored, one at the cave which had been the scene of the Saviour's birth; the other on the mount of His Ascension. For He who was 'God with us' had submitted to be born in a cave of the earth, and the place of His nativity was called Bethlehem by the Hebrews. Accordingly the pious empress honoured with rare memorials the scene of her travail who bore this heavenly

The shepherds' field, with Bethlehem in the background

Church of the Nativity, Bethlehem

Child, and beautified the sacred cave with all possible splen-dour."⁷ That Church of St. Helena, the Basilica of the Nativity, still stands, although it has suffered much through the centuries both from ravages and restoration. The Holy Cave is in the crypt below the floor of the sanctuary. The roof of the cave was removed to give place to the supports needed to sustain the weight of the building above. Nowadays two flights lead down to it, one of sixteen steps and the other of thirteen. The original walls and floor remain, now protected by slabs of marble. Into this marble is set a silver star with the inscription in Latin, "Here of the Virgin Mary Jesus Christ was born."

The limestone caves of Palestine have figured largely in the history of the country. It was to one of them that Lot and his daughters fled upon the destruction of Sodom and Gomorrha. Abraham bought a cave in Hebron as a burial place for Sara and, in the course of time, Abraham himself, Isaac and Rebecca, Jacob and Lia were interred there too. This family sepulchre of the patriarchs is venerated to the present day by Moslem and Christian — the Jew being rigorously excluded. When David fled from the jealousy of Saul, he and his men lived first in the caves of Adullam, and afterwards in the caves of Engaddi. As a boy in Bethlehem he would, of course, have been familiar with the caves of the district. Did the future king ever visit the cave in which the Son of David would be born long afterwards? It was in a cave of Horeb that the prophet Elias hid from the wrath of Queen Jezabel. To the present day there are caves under houses in Nazareth and Bethlehem. During most of his thirty-four years in Bethlehem St. Jerome lived and studied in a cave close to that cave which was the cradle of the Christian faith. He wrote: "I, too, miserable sinner that I am, have been accounted worthy to kiss the manger in which the Lord cried as a Babe, and to pray in the cave in which the travailing Virgin gave birth to the infant Lord."⁸

It seems clear from the remarks of Origen, quoted above, that the manger was still in the cave when he visited it. St.

Jerome saw it too, for he spoke of his privilege of kissing it. Apparently it was later removed, for he wrote sadly: "Alas! through a feeling of veneration for Christ, we have taken away the manger of clay to substitute for it one of silver. But how much more precious to me is that which has been removed. Silver and gold are the goods of the Gentiles; this crèche of clay (*luteum illud praesepium*) is of much more value for the Christian faith."[9] What was the nature of the manger? From St. Jerome's description it does not seem to have been made of wood, but of potter's clay which in Palestine is cheaper, more abundant, and easier to work.[10] Hence the manger was a kind of trough in which fodder was placed. This was the cradle of the infant Saviour. Unfortunately, it was stored away so safely in the troubled times that now it cannot be found. But some relics of the manger remain. In the year 640 the Arab armies of the Caliph Omar were in Palestine and had captured Jerusalem. The long night of Moslem misrule had fallen upon the Holy Land. During the reign of Pope Theodore I (642–649), a native of Jerusalem, some relics from the cave were brought to Rome for safety. These were five boards of sycamore wood that had been the supports of the manger. They are preserved in St. Mary Major's, and are now enclosed in an urn of silver and crystal, surmounted by a gilt figure of the Holy Child.[11]

What was in the manger? Not hay, for this, as we understand it, was not made in Palestine. "It is customary in Bible lands to cut or pull grass and other fodder plants, and give them to livestock. Women, with large back loads of such fodder, or donkeys similarly laden, may be seen any morning at the gates, or in the market places of the cities, where they offer it for sale. Large areas are sown in barley, vetch, clover, madick and other forage plants, to be cut and given to domestic animals in the spring and early summer. It is clear that it was also the custom in Bible days to cut grass for this purpose. But it is not customary to dry such cut grasses, as we do in making hay to be stored up as winter fodder, and there is no evidence that the Hebrews had such a custom. In fact, it would be out of place, as the winter is their season of green grass, and the flocks continue to crop the stubble to the end of the harvest season in midsummer; thereafter they find a scanty but sufficient pasturage until the early rains cause the 'tender grass' to sprout up with marvellous rapidity. Stall-fed animals have cut-grass mixed with their barley, and this seems to contain a considerable amount of nourishment and to answer the purpose of hay. Stall-fed milch cows are fed mainly on this fodder, and continue fat, and give milk on it."[12] Barley straw was the usual provender used in the stables of Solomon (cf. 3 Kings 4:28). "Will the wild ass bray when he hath grass? or will the ox low when he standeth before a full manger?" (Job 6:5.) "The Hebrew teben is the same as the Arabic tibn, which is the straw of wheat and barley cut by the threshing machine into pieces from one half to two inches long, and more or less split and torn, and mixed with chaff. It is the universal accompaniment to the provender of domestic herbiverous animals. It is usually mixed with barley, and takes the place of hay."[13] The straw provided for the use of animals became the bed for the Son of God.

Tradition has it that there were an ox and an ass in the cave. Isaias had said: "The ox knoweth his owner, and the ass his master's crib" (1:3). It has been suggested that this text has given rise to the tradition, but the cave was a stable, the natural place for such animals. The ass belonged to Joseph; the ox to some other traveller. One of the old Latin hymns (*De Nativitate Domini*) sings of the ox and the ass as warming the newly born Saviour with their breath. In Christian art, from the sixth century to the sixteenth, there is no picture of the Cave without these two animals. Sometimes the ox has been regarded as the symbol of the Jews, and the ass, of the Gentiles.

CHAPTER 13

The Virgin Birth

MARY must have shivered as she stepped into the darkness of the underground stable. At every step she had to hold up her long white tunic lest it be soiled by contact with the foulness of the floor. She held the lamp while Joseph cleared a space near the opening, near to what little air there was and away from proximity to the beasts at the back. The discomforts of the cave were real enough, but they were not intolerable. With loving and respectful hands Joseph made up a bed of straw for her near the entrance, but it would be a poor compliment to the prudence of both to suppose that she had to lie upon bare straw. Mary had been expecting to be confined in Bethlehem, and so she came provided with all the necessities which she could bring. Her foresight extended even to swaddling clothes, which she must have brought in her wallet, for they were unobtainable in the cave. Joseph unpacked their travelling requisites from the saddle-bags and laid them out on the manger.

We rejoice to think that Mary had a good bed upon which to lie, that is, judged by contemporary standards. For example, very poor people had no proper beds at all. "A bedstead of any pretensions was rare among the Hebrews, and was looked upon as a luxury."[1] The poor people simply lay on the floor or on the *leewan* and wrapped their large outer cloaks around them. This garment was the poor man's cloak by day and his coverlet by night, just as the ample plaid was to the Highlander of Scotland. Hence the Law commanded that, when this mantle was pawned or put in pledge for a loan, it should always be returned to its owner by sunset, lest he lack bed-clothes for the night. "But thou shalt restore it to him presently before the going down of the sun: that he may sleep in his own raiment and bless thee, and thou mayest have justice before the Lord thy God" (Deut. 24:13). Mary and Joseph were not so poor as to be compelled to pawn their garments.

"Amongst all classes the custom was to sleep in the day-clothes without any material change of garments; sheets were therefore superfluous. In its simplest form the bed consisted only of the day-clothes and the outer garment or cloak."[2] Again the Law refers to this custom in insisting on the timely return of the cloak. "For that same is the only thing wherewith he is covered, the clothing of his body, neither hath he any other to sleep in" (Exod. 22:27). But even in the cave Mary had a better bed than this. Over the straw she spread out the quilted caparison-cloth as a mattress and the stuffed saddle itself served as a pillow. From her wallet she produced a change of linen without which no one would travel far. It was a spare tunic, the long, white-sleeved undergarment reaching to the feet. Her goat-skin cloak would make a warm coverlet. So, by contemporary standards, Mary had a good bed in the cave and was comfortable enough.

The pious people of the period, encouraged by the Pharisees and rabbis, were sticklers for washing and purifications. Indeed the rabbis have drawn up an elaborate code on the practice. For example, it was strictly forbidden to eat "with common hands," that is, with unwashed hands (cf. Matt. 15:2). The rabbis admitted that the practice was not a Law of Moses, but a "tradition of the ancients." On that very account it was so strictly enjoined that to transgress the precept was regarded as a gross defilement which would lead to temporal destruction or at least to poverty. Bread eaten with unwashed hands was looked upon as filth. One rabbi who rejected this ordinance of the elders was buried in excommunication. The Saviour will enjoin His disciples to keep the Law of God rather than the ordinances of the elders, but His hour is not yet come. Mary and Joseph dared not disregard the precept lest they be excommunicated and cast out of the synagogue. So on their journey they carried with them the vessels for washing the hands before meals and the feet before retiring (cf. Cant. 5:3). "The Hebrews were accustomed to wash their hands in the manner which is now universal in the East, and which, whatever may be thought of its inconvenience, is unquestionably more refreshing and cleanly than washing in the water as it stands in a basin — which is a process regarded by Orientals with great disgust. The hands are therefore held over a basin, the use of which is only to receive the water which has been poured upon the hands from the jug or ewer which is held above them. This cannot very conveniently be managed without the aid of a servant or some other person. . . . The tesht and ibreeq are made of either metal or earthenware. The ibreeq is a waterjug, with a spout for the water to come through like a coffee-pot; from which the water is poured on the hands or feet, which are held over the basin. They are to be found in every Eastern house; they are used continually in the mornings. There are no washstands in the houses. The servant holds the tesht on the palm of his left hand and the ibreeq in the right hand, and a clean towel placed on his left shoulder for each person (cf. John 13:4), who washes his face and hands, taking the towel from off the servant's shoulder."[3]

As they were held in the hands during use, the tesht and ibreeq must have been small and portable. They could be wrapped in a towel and carried in the saddle-bags. The mire of unpaved roads in the East has to be seen to be believed, and as neither stockings nor socks were worn in sandals or open shoes, a wash for the feet was necessary before going to bed. For the convenience of the guests at the wedding of Cana, "there were set there six waterpots of stone, according to the manner of the purifying of the Jews, containing two or three measures apiece" (John 2:6). No khan would lack such facilities, for no pious guest would sit down to break bread without first washing his hands. So Joseph could fill his ewer with fresh water and provide Mary with an adequate supply even in the cave.

The cave was dark, for it had no window. Its sole illumination was light coming from the passage outside, and that must have been feeble even at midday, for the passage also was underground. Hence, anyone using the stable had to bring his lamp with him. A niche or ledge in the rocky wall provided a place for the lamp, as it does in the stone huts of the very poor to this day. Here Mary put her lamp, and in its light saw the grotesque shadows cast on the wall by the heads of the animals. The cave was dirty, cold, and dark, but she was clean, warm, and provided with a lamp. She was grateful when she could lie down on a good bed. The presence of the animals were inevitable, and she would not resent it. Furthermore, the warmth of their breath and bodies took the chill off the air.

Mary and Joseph said their night prayers together as usual. When Joseph rose to retire, the eloquent look with which Mary thanked him brought balm to his harassed heart. Outside in the passage he continued his prayers, but in silence, for he did not wish to attract attention by his voice or movements. So he sat down cross-legged and waited with Oriental patience. He would not sleep lest Mary should call upon him in vain. He was young, healthy, and warm enough in his heavy cloak, so a cold and wakeful night had no terrors for him. Overhead he heard the noise and movement cease, and the weary travellers seek their rest in the alcoves with the faint glimmer of a night-light in each. Soon the only sound to be heard was the slow munching of the contented animals. At midnight the silence was broken by the cry of a Baby.

And it came to pass that, when they were there, her days were accomplished, that she should be delivered. And she brought

*forth her first-born son, and wrapped him up in swaddling
clothes, and laid him in a manger, because there was no room
for them in the inn.*

These are the simple but solemn words in which the Nativity
is described in the canonical Gospel of St. Luke, and they bear
the very stamp of truth: they are a restrained "statement which
refutes the ravings of the apocryphal accounts," remarks St.
Jerome.[4] For example, the *Protoevangelium* contains a wild
story of St. Joseph rushing out to the town in search of a nurse.
When he came back with one, they were amazed to see the
cave filled with light, as if it were noonday, and to find Mary
sitting up with the Babe at her breast. When the astonished
midwife exclaimed: "Can this be true?" Mary is supposed to
have replied: "It is true; as there is no child like unto my Son,
so there is no woman like unto His Mother." But this account
is only a tale, and the arrogant answer is impossible from one
who described herself as "the handmaid of the Lord."

There was no nurse present. "No midwife assisted at His
birth," declared St. Jerome. "No woman's officiousness intervened. With her own hands she wrapped Him in swaddling
clothes, herself both mother and midwife."[5] Not even St. Joseph
is mentioned as being present at the birth. The canonical Gospel gives the impression that the Mother was able to attend to
the care of her Babe immediately, and the Fathers of the Church
have concluded that the birth was without pain as befitted the
Virgin-Mother. Surely the immaculate Mother of God was
exempt from the curse pronounced upon errant Eve: "In sorrow
shalt thou bring forth children" (Gen. 3:16). As the ripe fruit
gently parts from the parent branch, so was the Saviour born.
St. Cyprian says: "Instead of purple and king's linen, swaddling
bands and folded garments are got together: the Mother is the
midwife; to her beloved off-spring she proffers devoted homage;
she clasps, embraces, kisses and offers Him her breast, the whole
occupation full of delight: there is no pain, none of Nature's
offensiveness in her confinement."[5, 6] Bossuet contends: "He

comes forth like a shaft of light, like a ray of the sun; His Mother wonders to see Him appear all at once; this confinement is as free of cries as it is of pain and force; miraculously conceived, He is born more miraculously still, and the saints have found his being born even more wonderful than His being conceived of a virgin!"[7] Mary was able to rise from her bed to attend to the wants of her Child. With her own hands she wrapped Him up in swaddling clothes and laid Him in the manger. The Son of God was born. That was the all-engrossing, all-important fact. The long jolting journey down from Nazareth and her rude repulse by the boors of Bethlehem are of no consequence now. At last the Saviour is born and all is well.

> Gloomy night embrac'd the place
> Where the noble Infant lay.
> The Babe look't up and showed His face;
> In spite of darkness, it was day.
> It was Thy day, sweet; and did rise
> Not from the East, but from thine eyes.
>   — CRASHAW

The birth of Solomon is described, as if by himself, in the Book of Wisdom: "I myself also am a mortal man, like all others, and of the race of him, that was first made of the earth, and in the womb of my mother I was fashioned to be flesh. . . . And being born I drew in the common air, and fell upon the earth, that is made alike, and the first voice which I uttered was crying, as all others do. I was nursed in swaddling clothes, and with great cares. For none of the kings had any other beginning of birth" (7:1–). True, O Solomon the Wise, son of David; but you were born in the house of the king, your father, and your mother, Bethsabee, "the very beautiful," had troops of women to minister to her and to you! Bethsabee was a sinful woman; but Mary, the sinless one, brought forth the Son of David in a cave of the earth, alone and unattended.

What are swaddling bands? They are still in use in the East

and are very different from the little dresses or baby robes with sleeves in which Western infants are clothed. The Eastern infant was laid upon a square of cloth like a napkin, but spread diagonally. The upper corner was folded back to leave the head free, and the three other corners were folded over to enclose the whole body, including the arms and legs. Then the swaddling bands proper, which were rather like bandages, were wound outside the napkin and tied around the infant. The custom may have survived from early nomadic days when the people dwelt in the wilderness, for the bandaging not only afforded a protection against cold and a protection to the spine, but also enabled the mother to carry the infant more easily and securely. Of course, these swaddling bands had to be unloosed in attending to the child's needs, but it was usually kept confined in them until it began to use its limbs. During this period its skin was protected against chafing by being dusted with the powder of myrtle leaves, and any tender or sore places were rubbed with olive oil. Swaddling bands were usually made of plain linen or cotton, but well-to-do people had them made of embroidered stuffs.[8] The absence of these "clouts" or swaddling bands was a sign of the poverty or neglect of the parents (cf. Ezech. 16:4). Since Mary was neither poor nor neglectful, and was skilled in spinning and weaving, having been educated in the temple, it is probable that the swaddling clothes made by her own hands were of good linen and were tastefully embroidered. To this day the mothers of Bethlehem bind up their babies with linen strings with long fringes, by means of which they can carry them upon their backs or even hang them up out of the way![9] It was the custom to wash the newly born infant in water and to rub it with salt to make the limbs supple, and then to wrap it up in the linen napkin tied with swaddling bands. It is consoling to know that Mary herself was enabled to perform these intimate offices for her Child, and that the first human hands to touch the Word made Flesh were those of His Immaculate Mother.

"And the Word was made flesh, and dwelt among us" (John 1:14). How lovingly Mary clasped the Son of God to her breast! How tenderly she pressed His baby face to her cheek! The Messias was born: He was her Child: it was all true! Her eyes opened wide to feast her gaze upon Him; her lovely face blushed with the radiance of happy motherhood. St. Basil represents her as divided between love and adoration. She addresses the infant Saviour and says: "What am I to call You? A mortal? Not so, for I conceived You by divine operation. A God? But You have a human body. Ought I to come before You with incense, or to offer You my breast? Ought I to lavish upon You all the cares of a tender mother or to serve You with my forehead bowed down to the dust? O wonderful contrast! The heavens are Your abode, and yet I rock You upon my knee. You are upon earth, and yet You are not separated from the inhabitants of the celestial regions. The heavens are with You." Was she to adore Him as her God, or to love Him as her own flesh and blood? She did both.

The *Protoevangelium* would have us believe that St. Joseph went for a walk into the country while waiting for the Nativity. Is it credible that he, the divinely appointed guardian of both Child and Mother, would desert his post at such a time? Is it not most probable that he remained near at hand in the passage and within call? Then the *Protoevangelium* relates a marvellous phenomenon which is supposed to have occurred at the moment of the Nativity and which Joseph is supposed to have witnessed while out on this imaginary stroll. The phenomenon was nothing less than the sudden cessation of all movement around Bethlehem. The unknown author has the audacity to put his dramatic description in the mouth of St. Joseph himself: "Now I, Joseph, was walking, and I walked not. And I looked up into the air and saw the air in amazement. And I looked up into the pole of heaven and saw it standing still, and the birds of the air without motion. And I looked upon the earth and saw a dish set, and workmen lying by, and their hands were in the dish, and they that were chewing, chewed not, and they that were raising the food, raised it not, and they that put it to their mouth, put it not thereto; but the faces of all of them were looking upwards. And behold, there were sheep being driven, and they went not forward, but stood still; and the shepherd lifted his hand to smite them with his staff, and his hand remained up. And I looked upon the current of the river, and saw the mouths of the kids upon the water, and they drank not. And of a sudden all things moved forward in their course." This imaginary incident is as fabulous as a fairy tale, and indeed the climax of "The Sleeping Beauty" may be derived from it.

"Joseph!" When Mary called his name, he arose and entered the cave. Anxious, hoping, wondering, her best friend answered her call. In the dim light shed by the lamp from its ledge, he saw her kneeling by the manger, and he saw the white bundle encircled by her arms. When she turned her head at the sound of his steps, he saw that her eyes outshone the stars. One glimpse of that radiant face assured him that all was well, and humbly he thanked the Holy One, blessed be His Name. Another step and he was bending over her shoulder, and he saw Christ the Lord wrapped in swaddling clothes and laid in the manger, and falling down, he adored Him. Behind them the heads of the animals loomed up grotesquely and their warm breath rose up in the chill air of the cave. "The ox knoweth his master, and the ass the stable of his lord." The patient beasts of burden, the humble friends of man, had a place at the birth of the Lord of men and animals. But, after Mary His Mother, it was Joseph, her husband, guardian, and best friend, who had the honour of being the first to adore the Son of God made Man, and he deserved the honour.

The most ancient representation of the Nativity in existence is probably the fresco in the Catacomb of St. Priscilla in Rome. The Virgin-Mother is seated, holding her Child to her bosom, while a young man, standing by, points to a star overhead. It has been suggested that this figure represents the prophet Isaias, who had foretold that Emmanuel would be born of the Virgin. Really this does not seem very probable. More likely the figure represents Joseph, and in this, the very earliest picture extant of the Holy Family, he is depicted as quite a young man, without even a beard. De Rossi, the great Christian archaeologist, assigns the date of the fresco to the reign of Trajan or Hadrian, or, at the very latest, to the period of the Antonines, that is, during the second century.[10]

The Saviour was not only conceived in virginity, but also born in virginity. "Born of the Virgin Mary" is the solemn teaching of the Church. Mary retained her integrity in the birth of her Son. It was a miracle, of course, a special intervention of God in the laws of nature, "because no word shall be impossible with God." As Christ in His risen body will one day pass out of the sealed, stone tomb without opening it, so now He leaves the womb of His Mother and enters the world without depriving her of her virginity. St. Gregory of Nyssa wrote: "Although coming in the form of man, yet He is not subject in everything to the law of man's nature. While His being born of a woman tells of human nature, virginity becoming capable of child birth betokens something above man's nature. Of Him, then, His Mother's burden was light, the birth immaculate, the delivery without pain, the nativity without defilement. For as she, who by her guilt engrafted death into her nature, was condemned to bring forth in pain, it was fitting that she who brought Life into the world would accomplish her delivery with joy."[11] The pangs of childbirth, the sorrows of errant Mother Eve, were not for the immaculate Virgin-Mother. St. Augustine tersely expressed Catholic opinion: "She was a virgin before the birth, during the birth, and after the birth."[12] Thus all Christians confess "the Blessed Mary ever virgin." She alone is both virgin and mother; she alone is so blessed among women as to wear the crowns of maidenhood and motherhood, the double crown which no other daughter of Eve has ever worn or ever will wear.

The Nicene Creed, in its own stately fashion, states the doctrine for all Christians: "I believe in one God, the Father Almighty, Maker of heaven and earth, and of all things visible and invisible. And in one Lord Jesus Christ, the only-begotten Son of God, born of the Father before all ages. God of God; Light of Light; true God of true God; begotten, not made; being of one substance with the Father, by whom all things were made. Who for us men, and for our salvation, came down from heaven, and was incarnate by the Holy Ghost of the Virgin Mary, and was made man." The Baby born in the cave is God, the Second Person of the most august Trinity, the Maker of heaven and earth, omnipotent, eternal, immense, and immutable. The divine attributes can be predicated of a little child, for that Child is divine. "A mass of legend and literature," wrote the inimitable G. K. Chesterton, "has repeated and rung the changes on that single paradox; that the hands that made the sun and stars were too small to reach the huge heads of the cattle. Upon this paradox . . . all the literature of our faith is founded."[13]

Some seven centuries before Christ's coming, Isaias had expressed the same paradox by predicating divine attribute after attribute of a little Child: "For a child is born to us, and a son is given to us, and the government is upon his shoulder: and his name shall be called, Wonderful, Counsellor, God the Mighty, the Father of the world to come, the Prince of Peace" (9:6). St. Paul, too, expresses the paradox of our faith: "But when the fulness of the time was come, God sent his Son, made of a woman, made under the law" (Gal. 4:4). The God who made the world out of nothing is born of a woman, for of her He deigned to take His human nature. It is incredible, but it is true, and Jesus Christ was born in the stable of Bethlehem. Look, Christian, at Christ; look at God in the cave. Look at the wretched hole, the beasts, and the dirt. Look at the grave man, bent in wondering awe over Mother and Child, the faithful guardian of both. Look at the lovely girl-mother, with a light in her eyes that never shone in woman's eyes before. Look at the

Infant, look at Christ the Lord wrapped in swaddling clothes and laid in a manger. Look, Christian, and adore your Creator, your Redeemer, and your Judge.

> *Poor world (said I) what wilt thou do*
> *To entertain this starry stranger?*
> *Is this the best thou canst bestow?*
> *A cold, and not too cleanly manger?*
> *Contend, ye pow'rs of heav'n and earth*
> *To fit a bed for this huge birth.*
>
> *I saw the curl'd drops, soft and slow,*
> *Come hovering o'er the place's head;*
> *Off'ring their whitest sheets of snow*
> *To furnish the fair infant's bed.*
> *Forbear, said I, be not too bold.*
> *Your fleece is white, but 'tis too cold.*

— CRASHAW

CHAPTER 14

Angels and Shepherds

DARKNESS reigned over the Holy Land on that night of December 25. To the west the sea was black as pitch; beyond the Jordan to the east rolled the dark expanse of the plains; to the north the great bulk of Mount Hermon was shrouded in gloom; to the south the desert was clothed in invisibility. But within the girdle of darkness Palestine itself shone like a diamond on black velvet, for every house was lighted up. The illuminated towns were the facets of the jewel and the capital the brilliant centre. To the hosts of heaven, this one little land shone like an orb of light in a world of darkness.

Within the ring of its walls Jerusalem glowed refulgent. On its eastern hill the Temple blazed with lights; on the western hill Herod's palace was illuminated on the grand scale; the Tyropoean valley running from north to south flashed like a stream of fire. In the Upper City that girdled Mount Sion the palaces of the princes and prelates were lighted up, and in the huddle of hovels that ran down to the Dung Gate there was a light at every door. Lamps of all sizes were burning everywhere, from the gigantic candelabra of the Temple, of which the wicks were made from the used vestments of the priests, down to the tiny hand-lamp of the water-carrier's wife. Oil vendors, lamp sellers, and cheesemongers had been unusually busy that day. Since dusk began to fall the women were bustling about their

homes, cleaning and burnishing their old lamps, filling them
with oil, trimming the wicks, and sallying forth to buy new
lamps, supplies of oil, and also cheese for supper. As each
lamp was kindled by the woman of the house, the men folk
standing around recited the two benedictions: "Blessed be the
Lord our God, King of the Universe, who hast sanctified us by
Thy Commandments and enjoined us to enkindle the Hanukkah lamp," and "Blessed be the Lord our God, King of the
Universe, who has done wondrous things to our fathers in days
of yore at this season."[1]

Then the lamps were put into position for the night, not
inside the house to light up the chambers, but outside the doors
to illuminate the houses from without so that passers-by should
see them. The lamp was placed to the left of the door, as the
mezuzah was affixed to the right-hand door-post. The rabbis
disputed as to the number of lights to be used on the eight
nights of the feast of *Hanukkah*. The School of Hillel would
have begun the first night with the smallest number of lights
for each household and increase them nightly until, on the last
night, the number was eight times as many as on the first.
The School of Shammai would have the householders begin
with the largest number, thus reversing the process. One lamp
was sufficient for each household, but pious people preferred to
have a light for each member of the family, so that, according
to the more popular view of Hillel, if they enkindled five lamps
on the first night, they would have forty burning on the eighth.
Hence, the number of lamps in each town must have been
enormous.

Unlike the great pilgrimage festivals, the *Hanukkah* feast
could be celebrated everywhere, for the worshippers were not
obliged to travel up to Jerusalem. But, of course, in Jerusalem
itself all the adult males would attend the service in the Temple.
In the brilliantly illuminated courts, massed choirs of priests
chanted the verses of the Hallel (Psalms 112 and 117), and the
deep voices of many thousands of male voices thundered back

the responses, and the men waved palm branches in their hands until the long flames of the huge lamps wavered in the draught. Meanwhile, the women thronged the dairies situated in the Tyropoean Valley, which means "The Valley of the Cheese-mongers," where they bought cheese for supper. Women were encouraged to prepare a feast and make merry in their homes on the first night in memory of the heroic part played by Judith against the tyrant Holofernes on this night long ago. According to legend, she enticed him to eat largely of cheese and thus provoke a thirst, which he assuaged in deep potations of wine. When he fell into a drunken slumber, she had him at her mercy and the dire deed was done.[2]

Kislew is the ninth month of the Jewish calendar, but it corresponds roughly with our December. For example, in the last year of our Lord's life on earth it is reckoned that the 25th of Kislew corresponded with December 20.[3] But, as the *Hanuk-kah* celebrations lasted for eight nights, it is quite probable that the Holy Land was illuminated at the first Christmas. At the last feast of the Dedication, or *Hanukkah*, which He attended in Jerusalem, the Saviour spoke of Himself under the beautiful title of "The Good Shepherd," and described the tender relations between shepherd and flock (cf. John 10:11). On that occasion, the last anniversary on earth of His birth, did His thoughts go back to the shepherds who were summoned to His cradle in the manger? It was at this time, too, that He declared: "I am the light of the world" (John 9:5), at the cure of the man born blind. At the previous Feast of Tabernacles He had said the same thing (cf. John 8:12). These two feasts had much in common, for the ritual of both included the illumination of the Temple and the chanting of the Hallel during eight days. Thus, when He announced Himself under the magnificent title of "The Light of the World," He could point to the brilliant illumination of the Temple, and imply that while these lamps filled Jerusalem with light, He Himself was giving light to the whole world.

While it is true that neither the day nor the month of His Nativity is given by any evangelist, nevertheless it is remarkable that December 25, the date of the Feast of Lights, was fixed by the early Church as the birthday of the Saviour. The winter solstice is December 21, the shortest day of the year, after which daylight begins to lengthen. Before His coming the dark night of idolatry was spread over the earth. It was fitting that the "Light of the World" should have been born at that season of the year when the sun, in conflict with darkness, was beginning to extend its light in triumph. "On this day," wrote St. Gregory of Nyssa, "the darkness begins to diminish, and the light, taking on an increase, the night is driven back beyond its frontiers. It is not by chance that this happens at the same hour when He shines forth Who is the Light Divine of humanity. Nature, under this symbol, reveals a secret to those who are capable of comprehending it."[4]

At the first Christmas, however, the illuminations all over the Holy Land were not in honour of the birth of the Messias, for as yet His coming was not known. Bethlehem, as well as Jerusalem and other towns, was ablaze with lights in celebration of the second dedication of the Temple. "And it was the feast of the dedication in Jerusalem: and it was winter" (John 10:22). What was the origin of this feast? In the year 168 B.C., on the 25th day of the month of *Kislew*, the Temple had been desecrated and a pagan altar set up therein. This was the work of Antiochus Epiphanes, King of Syria, in an insane attempt to stamp out the worship of Jehovah. But within three years the mad despot was dead, and the heroic Hasmoneans had liberated the land and restored the true religion. On the third anniversary of the desecration, the 25th of *Kislew*, 165 B.C., Judas Machabeus had the Temple solemnly reconsecrated and the Feast of the Dedication established: "And Judas, and his brethren, and all the church of Israel decreed, that the day of the dedication of the altar should be kept in its season from year to year for eight days, from the five and twentieth day of the month of Casleu, with joy and gladness" (1 Mach. 4:29). The historian Josephus refers to this second dedication as "The Feast of Lights."[5] The rabbis ascribed the origin of the eight days' festival, with the custom of illuminating the houses to an alleged miracle. "This was that the one small cruse of consecrated oil found unpolluted by the Hasmonean priests when they entered the Temple, it having been sealed and hidden away, lasted for eight days until new oil could be prepared for the lamps of the holy candlestick."[6] For dedication the evangelist uses the Greek word *Enkainia,* and the rabbis the Hebrew word *Hanukkah.* In modern times it is celebrated as the feast of Jewish nationalism.

The service in the Temple was over and the people had departed to their homes, where they feasted and made merry until it was time to retire. But the lamps were left burning all night. Jerusalem must have presented a strange spectacle that night; the streets were silent and deserted but brilliantly illuminated by rows of lamps. The Chosen People were asleep. The vast courts of the Temple were empty, the only movements being made by the white-clad Levites on guard as they patrolled the enormous area in the brightness of the lamps. The priests of Jehovah were asleep. In his grand new palace on the other hill Herod the King lay fitfully tossing on his divan, for his bloated body was racked by the pain of his incurable disease. At length he, too, fell into the sleep of exhaustion. The elders of Israel, the doctors of the Law, the scribes and Pharisees, the leaders of the people, the wealthy merchants, the tired workmen, the women and children, were fast asleep that night. In Bethlehem itself, all the scions of David's kingly line were gathered together, but not to pay homage to the Prince of the House of David. They were assembled that they might be enrolled as the subjects of the foreign, pagan Caesar and pay him their tribute. Even they did not know that their Kinsman and Sovereign Lord was nigh, born in their midst, born in a stable, because there was no room for Him in their houses. The attention of the angels was fixed on earth that night as never before.

But the hosts of heaven disregarded the King's palace, for the Messias was not there. They were indifferent even to the lighted Temple, for He was not in His Father's house. The attention of Cherubim and Seraphim was focussed on the dark cave of Bethlehem with its one poor lamp burning on the wall, for Christ the Lord was there.

Was anyone in Israel awake that night? The poor shepherds keeping watch over the flocks of their employers are the only ones mentioned in the Gospel. Jehovah will send His angels to summon some of His Chosen people to pay homage to His newly born Son. He will choose, not the King from the palace, nor the priests from the Temple, nor the learned nor the wise nor the wealthy, but the simple shepherds from the fold. Theirs will be the privilege of representing the chosen people at the cradle of the Messias. It is well. Their humble homage will be in keeping with the humility of the coming of the Saviour. "But the foolish things of the world hath God chosen, that he may confound the wise; and the weak things of the world hath God chosen . . . and things that are not, that he might bring to nought things that are: that no flesh should glory in his sight" (1 Cor. 1:27-29). The rabbis regarded the shepherds as the basest and most foolish class of the community, the very dregs of society, for they disregarded the minute regulations prescribed to ensure liturgical purity. Indeed, their wild and unsettled manner of life, moving with their flocks from pasturage to pasturage, prevented them from complying with the elaborate ordinances of the rabbis. They were so ignorant that no court of justice would accept their testimony, and they were placed on the same footing as the heathen whom it was forbidden to succour.[7] These poor nomads were badly fed, badly housed, and badly paid.

Jacob had been employed as a shepherd by his kinsman Laban, and complained bitterly of the arduous life: "Have I therefore been with thee twenty years? thy ewes and goats were not barren, the rams of the flock I did not eat: Neither did

I shew thee that which the beast had torn, I made good all the damage: whatsoever was lost by theft, thou didst exact it of me. Day and night was I parched with heat, and with frost, and sleep departed from my eyes. And in this manner have I served thee in thy house twenty years, fourteen for thy daughters, and six for thy flocks: thou hast changed also my wages ten times. Unless the God of my father Abraham, and the fear of Isaac had stood by me, peradventure now thou hadst sent me away naked: God beheld my affliction and the labour of my hands, and rebuked thee yesterday" (Gen. 31:38–42). Exploited by his employer, exposed to extremes of heat and cold, never sure of a full night's rest, in peril from robbers and beasts of prey, with losses deducted from his scanty wages, the shepherd's lot was not a happy one.

> *In summer's heat, and winter's cold,*
> *He fed his flock, and penn'd the fold.*

Bethlehem was situated not far from a desert, not a vast, sandy, treeless, waterless plain like the burning Syrian desert, but a tract of waste land sloping down to the Jordan valley. After the winter rains there would be "much grass in the place," as St. John said of a rather similar desert in the north of the country (6:10). Poor pasturage it was, but good enough for the hardy sheep of Palestine, which can subsist where our sheep would starve. It was in this very desert that David had watched his father's flock and had killed the lion and the bear that had raided the fold (cf. 1 Kings 17:34).

The sheep of Palestine have not changed much since the days of our Saviour. The small, active sheep have tawny heads with long ears drooping like a spaniel's, white fleeces, and broad, fat tails. Only the rams have horns. The tails are so large that they often weigh as much as a third of the total weight of the animal. When the skinned carcass is seen hanging in a butcher's stall, the size of the tail surprises the stranger. Its fat has always been considered a delicacy. Being one of the best parts of the beast, it was set apart to be offered to Jehovah, and so the priest officiating at the sacrifice was ordered to cut it off.

Pictures representing the shepherds watching over their flocks in the open air of the fields do not correspond with reality. Even in summer it was the custom to herd the sheep into the fold for the night, because of the danger of robbers and wild beasts. In the cold, wet season from November to March the sheep were shut up, not merely in the open yard of the fold, but under cover of its roof. So on the first Christmas night it is not likely that the flocks were lying out in the open, exposed to the inclement weather and the danger of robbers. "The country above us has ever been a favourite range for sheep and goats. Those low, flat buildings out on the sheltered side of the valley are sheepfolds. They are called marah, and, when the nights are cold, the flocks are shut up in them, but in ordinary weather they are merely kept within the yard. This, you observe, is defended by a wide stone wall, crowned all around with sharp thorns, which the prowling wolf will rarely attempt to scale. The nimer, however, and fahed—the leopard and panther of this country—when pressed with hunger, will overleap this thorny hedge, and with one tremendous bound land among the frightened fold. Then is the time to try the nerve and heart of the faithful shepherd. . . . Though there are now no lions here, there are wolves in abundance; and leopards and panthers, exceeding fierce, prowl about these wild wadies. They not infrequently attack the flock in the very presence of the shepherd, and he must be ready to do battle at a moment's warning. I have listened with intense interest to their graphic descriptions of downright and desperate fights with these savage beasts. And when the thief and the robber come (and come they do), the faithful shepherd has often to put his life in his hand to defend his flock. I have known more than one case in which he had literally to lay it down in the contest. A poor faithful fellow last spring, between Tiberias and Tabor, instead of fleeing, actually fought three Bedawin robbers until he was hacked to pieces with their khanjars, and died among the sheep he was defending."[8]

Since the shepherds and their flocks could not have been lying out under the inclement skies of a winter night, where, then, was their sheepfold? The authority of no less a person than St. Jerome fixes the precise spot for us. In the year 404 he wrote from Bethlehem to console Eustochium for the loss of her mother, the noble lady Paula. He describes how Paula came to Bethlehem and venerated the manger in the cave: "After this Paula went a short distance down the hill to the Tower of Edar, that is, 'of the flock,' near where Jacob fed his flocks, and where the shepherds keeping watch by night were privileged to hear the words 'Glory to God in the highest; and on earth peace to men of good will.' While they were keeping their sheep they found the Lamb of God." St. Jerome gives further indication that the Flock Tower was about a thousand paces, a Roman mile, from Bethlehem,[9] and that it was situated to the east of the town.[10]

The place was historic since the time of Jacob, and preserved its name through the centuries, for it was a Chanaanite sanctuary as well as a watch tower. Long before the Nativity there was a tradition that the coming of the Messias would be proclaimed at this spot, as did actually happen. Half an hour's walk from Bethlehem to the east brings one to a place named Kirbet Siar el Ghanem, "the Ruins of the Sheepcot." Modern excavation has revealed the remains of a church with three aisles. This was the first monastery founded in Palestine, and its title was "The Sheepfold." It contains the traditional burial place of the Three Shepherds. At a short distance from the building, the base of a square tower, each side of which was eighteen feet long, was discovered. This is believed to be the vestiges of the Flock Tower. About the year 385 St. Sylvia of Acquitaine visited near Bethlehem "the church ad Pastores." She wrote: "There one sees a very well lighted cavern which encloses an alter, at the very place where the angel appeared to the shepherds while they were watching, and announced to them the Birth of Christ."[11] Thus this site corresponds better than any other with the descriptions left by early pilgrims.

On the night of the first Christmas eve the rocky hillock was enveloped in darkness. At its base there was a crescent-shaped cavern with a wide mouth facing north, making it well lighted by day. Its dimensions were about sixty-five feet in width and about forty-five feet in depth. It was approached by a gentle ascent from the fields below. The tower on the summit of the rock in daylight commanded an extensive view of the surrounding sheep walks.[12] The long, open front of the cavern was doubtless protected by the customary stone wall. The entrance could have been a gate or, more likely, closed up with piled-up bushes of thorn.

The traditional number of the shepherds on guard is three, and all would be within the fold, for the darkness of night would not warrant stationing a man in the watch-tower. As the night was cold, they would have lighted a fire from a pile of thorny brushwood. Behold them, then, squatting around their fire in the cavern, warming their bare legs, with their rough sheepskin mantles worn with the fleece next to the body pulled closely around their shoulders, and their staffs and slings laid close at hand, ready to start up at the first hint of danger. Their unkempt, shaggy dogs lay at their feet near the thorn-filled gap, blinking their eyes in the light of the fire, but with ears alert to catch the first sound of danger. As the sheep were trained to follow the shepherd, these dogs were not kept to drive the sheep, as our collies are, but rather to sound the alarm at the approach of danger. The sheep filled the rest of the commodious cavern. There were no lambs as yet in the flock, for it was too early for the lambing season. It is easy to picture this simple, pastoral scene in the cavern: the shepherds chatting or dozing over the fire with their dogs at their feet, and the white mass of animals behind in the darkness, snug, warm, and sheltered from wind and rough weather. Outside all was dark and still. Within

the cave the red firelight flickered on the smoke-blackened walls
and the many rounded backs of the sheep.

*And there were in the same country shepherds watching, and
keeping the night-watches over their flock. And behold an angel
of the Lord stood by them, and the brightness of God shone
round about them, and they feared with a great fear.*

Where, precisely, did the first angel appear? Within the wall
of the sheepfold, just beside them, for we are told that he
"stood by them." From their situation inside the cavern they
could not have seen him if he had "dropt from the zenith like
a falling star" upon the fields outside. Their first intimation of
his presence was his appearance as he "stood by them, and the
brightness of God shone round about them," in such a blaze of
celestial splendour that darkness seemed turned into daylight.
This brilliance was not evanescent like a flash of lightning, but
as steady as the noonday sun. The red, leaping flame of their
fire seemed to sink and fade as if strong sunlight beat upon it.
Every stone in the rough wall of the fold and every tuft of
wool upon the backs of the sheep seemed to stand out distinctly.
The shepherds suddenly looked up to find an angel of God
standing beside them in the cavern. No wonder they feared as
they looked upon him, glorious, benignant, and beautiful, the
messenger of the Most High.

What was the angel like in appearance? Being a pure spirit,
he had to assume some bodily form in order to become visible
to mortal eyes. Like other angels upon previous manifestations,
he probably took a human form and appeared like a man. Abraham and Manoah had mistaken angels for mere men (cf. Gen.
18:2; Judges 13:6). After the Resurrection Mark says that the
women saw at the tomb "a young man sitting on the right side,
clothed with a white robe" (16:5). Luke adds that "two men
stood by them, in shining apparel" (24:4), and Matthew says
of the angel who rolled back the stone that "his countenance
was as lightning, and his raiment as snow" (28:3).

What was the name of the angel who spoke to the shepherds? Luke tells us that Gabriel was the Angel of the Annunciation, but he does not mention the name of the Angel of the Nativity. Perhaps it is revealed by John. He tells of "a great sign in heaven" (Apoc. 12:1) how, when the "woman clothed with the sun, and the moon under her feet, and on her head a crown of twelve stars," was about to be delivered of her Child, "a great red dragon" appeared ready to "devour her Son" when he should be born. "And there was a great battle in heaven: Michael and his angels fought with the dragon . . . and that great dragon was cast out, that old serpent, who is called the devil and Satan." If Michael and his angels were the champions of the Child and His Mother, very likely it was they who were the heralds of the Nativity in Bethlehem. Behold, then, Michael the Archangel as he stood in the sheepfold, in the guise of a young man clothed with a white robe, but his angelic nature shone through the veils of the flesh and made his face luminous as lightning, his very raiment white as snow, so that his shining apparel dazzled the eyes of the shepherds. Is it any wonder that "they feared with a great fear"? How could they have known that this glorious Being was not Jehovah Himself? Others before them had mistaken an angel for the Most High: "We shall certainly die, because we have seen God," ejaculated the parents of Samson at the sight of an angel (Judges 13:22). From the golden glory the clear tones of the angelic voice rang out like a chiming bell to reassure them:

> *Fear not; for, behold, I bring you good tidings of great joy, that shall be to all the people. For this day is born to you a Saviour, who is Christ the Lord, in the city of David.*

Did they understand? Of course they did. Wild, ignorant men though they were, the shepherds could not misunderstand the significance of the phrase "Christ the Lord," for the words were a popular description of the expected Messias. Besides, this was Bethlehem, the city of David, the very place where He was expected to be born. Good tidings, great news indeed, the very best they had ever heard! Now they understand why the skies without are illuminated, and that the great being beside them is the herald of His Master. And the great voice pealed on over their heads bowed in awe:

And this shall be a sign unto you: You shall find the infant wrapped in swaddling clothes, and laid in a manger.

The word "manger" gave them the clue whereby they could find the Messias. Being shepherds they were familiar with the stables of the locality, and they knew of the one with the manger in it. Perhaps they had previously used it themselves. The idea of a birth in a cave would be less startling to these primitive herdsmen than to more civilised townsmen. "Swaddling clothes" would also mean something to these men. Their own wives carried their babies from pasture to pasture wrapped up like little mummies in swaddling bands. So the Messias was come as a baby, not like the Lion of the fold of Juda. They feared and hated lions, their natural enemies, whereas a little, helpless infant inspired them with pity and affection. But who ever expected the Messias to be born in a stable? Unlike the learned Zachary, these unsophisticated men had no hesitation in accepting the word of an angel. The heavenly voice ceased. Then such a torrent of melody poured out of the skies that the shepherds looked across the wall in amazement.

And suddenly there was with the angel a multitude of the heavenly army, praising God, and saying: Glory to God in the highest; and on earth peace to men of good will.

The shepherds looked out of their folds and saw, not one, but thousands of angels. Heaven's own choir turned out to sing the carol of a Child cradled in a manger! The cavern opening faced the north. Over the snow-clad fields below, over the hill of Mar Elias that intervened and hid Jerusalem from them, they saw the hosts of heaven deploy their brilliant ranks. The whole landscape was lit up with the splendour of legions of

angels. Over the Flock Tower above their heads, over the bare
fields, over the flat roofs of the town, over the hills of Bethlehem
circled the glittering choirs of heaven and the exquisite voices
of angels sang the triumphant strains of "Gloria in excelsis Deo!"

The presence of the angels was as real as the presence of
the shepherds. In Bethlehem two worlds met — the supernatural
and the natural, and one was as real as the other. The invisible
King of the unseen realms of heaven took a visible form upon
earth, and hosts of his heavenly creatures came visibly to adore
Him. After the birth itself, no incident of that memorable night
has so impressed the minds of Christians as the inrush of the
angels over the fields of Bethlehem. Unbelievers, while accepting the Babe, the Mother, the shepherds, and the cave, are inclined to reject the supernatural glory become visible overhead.
But historically the supernatural is as much part of the scene as
the natural. Our view of the picture becomes wrong, incomplete,
out of focus, if we have eyes for the natural alone. The appearance upon earth of God's heavenly creatures is less a wonder
than the coming of God Himself.

When the foundations of the earth were laid, "the morning
stars praised me together, and all the sons of God made a joyful
melody" (Job 38:7). But the angels had greater cause for re-
joicing when God became Man on earth. And rejoice they did
in their thousands. So many of them appeared over Bethlehem
that they are described as "a multitude of the heavenly army."
The royal psalmist had cried out: "Praise ye the Lord from the
heavens: praise ye him in the high places. Praise ye him, all
his angels: praise ye him, all his hosts" (148:1-2). Daniel declared: "Thousands of thousands ministered to him, and ten
thousand times a hundred thousand stood before him" (7:10).
If so many attend the Ancient of Days as He sits in judgment,
why not as many to celebrate His coming on earth? Isaias had
declared: "In the year that King Ozias died, I saw the Lord
sitting upon a throne high and elevated: and his train filled
the temple. Upon it stood the seraphims: the one had six wings,

and the other had six wings: with two they covered his face, and with two they covered his feet, and with two they flew. And they cried one to another, and said: Holy, holy, holy, the Lord God of hosts, all the earth is full of his glory. And the lintels of the doors were moved at the voice of him that cried, and the house was filled with smoke" (6:1-4). This was the splendid vision which the great prophet saw in the House of God, but the poor shepherds saw something more wonderful still: the Lord of Hosts as an Infant in a stable.

> *Glory to God in the highest;*
> *And on earth peace to men of good will.*

That is what the angels sang. It is a verse of Hebrew poetry, two lines, two parallel sentiments: glory to God and peace to men. The word here translated as "good will" signifies in the original the good pleasure of God in men rather than the good will of men towards God. The Nativity of His only-begotten Son gives to God infinite glory, worthy of His divine majesty. To men upon earth it brings peace, if they are pleasing to God. Peace from the Prince of Peace, peace of mind and heart and soul here below in the service of God, and hereafter eternal peace in heaven. "And the peace of God, which surpasseth all understanding, keep your hearts and minds in Christ Jesus" (Phil. 5:7).

> *And it came to pass, after the angels departed from them into heaven, the shepherds said one to another: Let us go over to Bethlehem, and let us see this word that is come to pass, which the Lord hath shewed to us. And they came with haste; and they found Mary and Joseph, and the infant lying in the manger.*

The shepherds hastened to see the Messias. They had not far to go, for Bethlehem was less than a mile from the Flock Tower. When the yawning keeper of the khan opened his gates at dawn, he was surprised to find three shepherds waiting outside in the cold morning air. When he let them in, they hastened across the crowded courtyard and down the steps to the stables.

They saw the lamp still burning dimly on its ledge, they saw the ox and the ass, they saw the solemn Joseph, the radiant girl-mother, and they saw "Christ the Lord wrapped in swaddling clothes and laid in the manger."

To whom did the shepherds tell their good tidings? Naturally the travellers in the khan first heard the news, and then the townsfolk of Bethlehem and the strangers come up for the census. The evangelist does not tell us that anyone except the shepherds had seen the glory of the singing angels in the skies. It is not likely that Mary and Joseph saw the splendid vision, for they were half-underground in the cave behind the khan. It is true that the social position of the shepherds was very low and that they were despised as unworthy of credence by the rabbis. But if they did not open their mouths in the synagogues, they could speak in the market place, the sheep folds, and the wine shops. They could not keep silent about the most wonderful sight of their lives and about the momentous news that the Messias at last had come.

As the word went round on the first Christmas morning, the curious came to stare at the Child and His Mother. They saw nothing spectacular, nothing of the pomp and circumstance which the legend of the Messias as a warrior King had led them to expect. Neither did they see one single angel. So they shook their heads and departed, blaming themselves for having listened to the idle tales of silly shepherds. Even the best people are slow to believe in any manifestation of the supernatural. Did anyone in Lourdes at first believe little Bernadette? Not even her own parents! Did anyone in Fatima believe the three children until the solar phenomenon crushed their incredulity? "And all that heard, wondered: and at those things that were told them by the shepherds." The evangelist says that their hearers wondered, not that they believed. But there were two people in Bethlehem who believed every word of the shepherds. We can imagine how carefully Joseph questioned them upon every detail of the vision, with what breathless interest Mary hung upon their words. How she must have treasured it all up and pondered in her heart over all these words in the future!

The testimony of the shepherds received so little general credence that it was not reported to Herod. Herod first heard of the Nativity much later, when the Magi came riding into Jerusalem and asked the question: "Where is He that is born King of the Jews?" Yet Herod employed a vast number of secret police to keep his subjects under strict supervision and to detect any hint of possible conspiracies. The historian Josephus relates: "Nor did he permit the citizens either to meet together, or to walk, or eat together, but watched everything they did, and when any were caught, they were severely punished; and many there were who were brought to the citadel Hyrcania, both openly and secretly, and were there put to death; and there were spies set everywhere, both in the city and in the roads, who watched those who met together."[13] Naturally the spies were particularly vigilant on the occasion of the unpopular census when people from different parts of the kingdom met together in groups and were likely to express their political opinions. If a spy in Bethlehem had attached any importance to what the shepherds said, he would have hastened to the palace with the news and a maniple of soldiers would have descended upon Bethlehem. But nothing of the sort seemed to have happened, so the story of the shepherds must have been discredited.

Who were the employers of the poor shepherds? Who were the owners of the flocks committed to their care? The flocks pastured around the Flock Tower were destined for sale, not in the public market, but in the bazaars of the Temple courts. The lambs were not destined to become food for men, but sacrifice to God. The Lamb of God was born beside the sacrificial sheep. Such a coincidence has a deep symbolical significance. The owners of these Temple sheep were the clique of priestly aristocrats who controlled the Temple market for their own profit. The immense wealth of these chief priests was derived, in part at least, from their monopoly of the sale of sacrificial requisites in the Temple courts, later to become known as the "Bazaars of the sons of Annas." But this infamous Annas, father-in-law of the still more infamous Caiaphas, was not yet High Priest, for he was not appointed until the year A.D. 6 or 7. At this time the head of the firm which owned the sheep and employed the shepherds was the High Priest Joazar, Herod's willing tool in persuading the people to submit to the census. Any sheep found wandering in the vicinity of the Flock Tower was presumed to belong to the Temple flocks. The males were offered as burnt-offerings, and the females as peace-offerings. To encourage people to bring up such strays for sacrifice, the finders were remitted the price of the concomitant drink-offerings, which in their case was defrayed by the Temple treasury. Later on Rabbi Jehudah decreed concerning such wandering sheep: "If suitable for Passover sacrifices, they are Passover sacrifices, provided it be not more than thirty days before the feast."[14]

It was in the neighbourhood of the Flock Tower of Bethlehem that the shepherds found the Lamb of God who was destined to become a sacrifice at a future Passover for the lost sheep of the House of Israel. "But this is not all. It is when we remember, that presently these shepherds would be in the Temple, and meet those who came thither to worship and to sacrifice, that we perceive the full significance of what otherwise would have seemed scarcely worth while noticing in connection with humble shepherds: 'And when they had seen it, they made known abroad the saying which was told them concerning this child. And all they that heard it wondered at those things which were told them by the shepherds' (Luke 2:17, 18). Moreover, we can understand the wonderful impression made on these in the courts of the Temple, as, while they selected their sacrifices, the shepherds told the devout of the speedy fulfilment of all these types in what they had themselves seen and heard in that night of wonders; how eager, curious crowds might gather around to discuss, to wonder, perhaps to mock; how the heart of 'Just and devout' old Simeon would be gladdened within him, in expectation of the near realisation of a life's hopes and prayers; and how aged Anna, and they who like her 'looked for redemption in Israel,' would lift up their heads, since their salvation was drawing nigh. Thus the shepherds would be the most effectual heralds of the Messiah in the Temple, and both Simeon and Anna be prepared for the time when the infant Saviour would be presented in the sanctuary. But there is yet another verse which, as we may suggest, would find a fuller explanation in the fact that these shepherds tended the Temple flocks. When in Luke 2:20 we read that 'the shepherds returned, glorifying and praising God,' the meaning in that connection seems somewhat difficult till we realise that, after bringing their flocks to the Temple, they would return to their own homes, and carry with them, joyfully and gratefully, tidings of the great salvation."[15]

It was the shepherds and not their masters who were summoned to the cradle of the Messias. O happy shepherds, more privileged than king or priest or rabbi! With your ears you have heard the song of the Seraphim and with your own eyes you have seen the Lord of Hosts. "Blessed are the eyes that see the things which you see. For I say to you, that many prophets and kings have desired to see the things that you see, and have not seen them; and to hear the things that you hear, and have not heard them" (Luke 10:23–24).

References

CHAPTER 1

1. Thomson, *The Land and the Book*, xxxviii.
2. Hastings, *Dictionary of the Bible*, "City"; "Gate."
3. Lagrange, *Évangile selon Saint Luc.*
4. *Jewish Encyclopedia*, "Shophar."

CHAPTER 2

1. Papini, Giovanni, *Life of Christ*, trans. D. C. Fisher (New York: Harcourt, Brace and Co., 1923), 26.
2. Gibbon, *The Decline and Fall of the Roman Empire*, I, 3.
3. *The Annals*, I, 11.
4. Claudianus, *De Consulatu Stilichonis*, 3, 1.
5. Curtius, *De rebus gestis Alexandri Magni*, 9, 3.
6. Eusebius, *The Church History*, I, 7.
7. Ollivier, *De Bethléem à Nazareth*, 2, 1.

CHAPTER 3

1. *Epistle 129.*
2. *The Life of Josephus*, 45.
3. *The Jewish War*, 3, 3, 2.
4. *Ibid.*, 6, 9, 3.
5. *Ibid.*, 2, 14, 3.
6. Felten, *Storia dei Tempi del Nuovo Testamento*, 1, 1.
7. Sanday and Waterhouse, *Sacred Sites of the Gospels* (Oxford: The Clarendon Press), I.
8. *The Jewish Antiquities*, 14, 7, 3.
9. *The Church History*, I, 6.
10. *Op. cit.*, 14, 11, 6.
11. Jones, *The Herods of Judaea* (Oxford University Press, 1938), 1.
12. *Op. cit.*, 15, 6, 6.

CHAPTER 4

1. *The Jewish Antiquities*, 15, 9, 3.
2. *Ibid.*, 18, 1, 1.
3. *The Life of Josephus*, 1.

CHAPTER 5

1. *The Land and the Book*, xxvii.
2. *Jewish Encyclopedia*, "Fuel."
3. *Ibid.*, "Coal."
4. Reprinted by permission of Dodd, Mead & Co., from *In the Steps of the Master*, 5, by H. V. Morton. Copyright, 1934, by Dodd, Mead & Co., Inc.
5. Vigouroux, *Dictionnaire de la Bible*, "Feu."
6. *Ibid.*, "Four." Smith, *Dictionary of the Bible*, "Oven."
7. Vigouroux, *op. cit.*, "Lampe."
8. Hastings, *Dictionary of the Bible*, "Day's Journey."
9. *De Sancta Virginitate*, 4.
10. Singer, *The Authorised Daily Prayer Book of the United Hebrew Congregations*.

CHAPTER 6

1. Hastings, *Dictionary of the Bible*, "Numbers," "Hours," "Years."
2. Talmud, *Berakoth*.
3. *Dictionary of Christ and the Gospels*, "Cock-Crowing."
4. Talmud, *op. cit.*
5. *Ibid.*
6. Cf. O'Shea, *Mary and Joseph* (Milwaukee: The Bruce Publishing Co., 1949), 316–319.
7. Thomson, *The Land and the Book*, xxx.
8. *Dictionary of Christ and the Gospels*, "Bread."
9. *The Jewish Antiquities*, 17, 6, 5.
10. Thomson, *op. cit.*, v.
11. Talmud, *Yoma*.
12. *The Annals*, I, 17.
13. O'Shea, *op. cit.*, 92.
14. *Dictionary of Christ and the Gospels*, "Dress."
15. Thomson, *op. cit.*, xxiv.
16. Vigouroux, *Dictionnaire de la Bible*, "Bourse."
17. *Jewish Encyclopedia*, "Bareheadedness."
18. Talmud, *Shabbath*.
19. Talmud, *Pirke Aboth*.

CHAPTER 7

1. Hastings, *Dictionary of the Bible*, "Ass."
2. *Jewish Encyclopedia*, "Etiquette."
3. Hastings, *op. cit.*, "Key."
4. Thomson, *The Land and the Book*, vii.
5. *Ibid.*, x.
6. *The Jewish Antiquities*, 8, 13, 8.
7. Hastings, *Dictionary of the Bible*, "Dog."
8. Smith, *Dictionary of the Bible*, "Dog."
9. Vigouroux, *Dictionnaire de la Bible*, "Engannim."
10. Ricciotti, *The Life of Christ*, trans. Zizzamia (Milwaukee: The Bruce Publishing Co., 1947), 239.

CHAPTER 8

1. *Dictionary of Christ and the Gospels,* "Samaritan."
2. Talmud, *Berakoth.*
3. Smith, *Dictionary of the Bible,* "Samaria."
4. *The Jewish War,* 4, 8, I.
5. Smith, *op. cit.,* "Shechem."
6. *Ibid.*
7. *Dictionary of Christ and the Gospels,* "Samaritan."
8. Hastings, *Dictionary of the Bible,* "Sycamore."
9. Smith and Cheetham, *Dictionary of Christian Antiquities,* "St. Joseph"; Jameson, *Legends of the Madonna.*
10. Vigouroux, *Dictionnaire de la Bible,* "Pont"; "Casphin."
11. Hastings, *op. cit.,* "Ford."

CHAPTER 9

1. Meistermann, *Guide to the Holy Land* (New York: P. J. Kenedy & Sons, 1924), xv.
2. Thomson, *The Land and the Book,* xvi.
3. Edersheim, *The Temple, Its Ministry and Services* (New York: Fleming H. Revell Co., 1926), I.
4. *The Jewish War,* 5, 2, 2.
5. Vigouroux, *Dictionnaire de la Bible,* "Citerne."
6. *The Jewish Antiquities,* 4, 8, 37.
7. Tissot, *The Life of Our Lord Jesus Christ,* ii.
8. *Op. cit.,* 5, 4, 3.

CHAPTER 10

1. *Dictionary of Christ and the Gospels,* "Jerusalem."
2. Thomson, *The Land and the Book,* xx.
3. *The Jewish War,* 4, 8, 3.
4. *The New Jerusalem* (New York: Doubleday & Co., Inc., 1921), iii.
5. Graf, *In Christ's Own Country* (London: Burns, Oates & Washburne, 1937), vii.
6. G. A. Smith, *Jerusalem,* I, 5.
7. *Op. cit.,* 5, 3, 2.
8. Smith, *Dictionary of the Bible,* "Gehenna."
9. Hastings, *Dictionary of the Bible,* "Terebinth."
10. Guérin, *La Judée,* I.
11. *The Jewish Antiquities,* 15, 9, 4.
12. *Epistle* 108.
13. Meistermann, *Guide to the Holy Land* (New York: P. J. Kenedy & Sons, 1924), iv.

CHAPTER 11

1. *The Gospel of Jesus Christ* (London: Burns, Oates & Washburne, Ltd., 1938), I.
2. *Commentaria in Quatuor Evangelia.*
3. *Commentarii in Quatuor Evangelistas.*

4. *The Life and Teaching of Jesus Christ* (London: Burns, Oates & Washburne, Ltd., 1934).

5. *Vie de Notre-Seigneur Jésus Christ,* I, 3.

6. *The Christ the Son of God* (New York: Longmans, Green and Co., 1919), I, 4.

7. Ricciotti, *The Life of Christ* (Milwaukee: The Bruce Publishing Co., 1947), 241.

8. Vigouroux, *Dictionnaire de la Bible,* "Innocents"; Fillion, *op. cit.,* I, 4.

9. *The Jewish War,* 3, 3, 2.

10. Eusebius, *The Church History,* 3, 20.

11. Edersheim, *The Life and Times of Jesus the Messiah* (New York: Longmans, Green and Co., 1925), I, 2, 1.

12. *The Land and the Book,* xxix.

13. O'Shea, *Mary and Joseph* (Milwaukee: The Bruce Publishing Co., 1949), 5.

14. Vigouroux, *op. cit.,* "Caravansérail."

15. *Ibid.,* "Chamaan."

16. *The Life of Our Lord Jesus Christ,* I.

17. Prat, *Jesus Christ,* trans. Heenan (Milwaukee: The Bruce Publishing Co., 1951), I, 82.

18. Talmud, *Pirke Aboth.*

CHAPTER 12

1. Hastings, *Dictionary of the Bible,* "Bethlehem."

2. Vigouroux, *Dictionnaire de la Bible,* "Bethléem."

3. *Ibid.,* "Caravansérail."

4. *Trypho,* 78.

5. *Contra Celsum,* I, 51.

6. *Epistle* 58.

7. *The Life of Constantine,* 3, 43.

8. *Epistle* 108.

9. *Dictionnaire Pratique des Connaissances Religieuses,* "Bethléem."

10. Vigouroux, *op. cit.,* "Crèche."

11. Smith and Cheetham, *Dictionary of Christian Antiquities,* "Manger."

12. Hastings, *op. cit.,* "Hay."

13. *Ibid.,* "Straw."

CHAPTER 13

1. *Dictionary of Christ and the Gospels,* "Bed."

2. Hastings, *Dictionary of the Bible,* "Bed."

3. *Dictionary of Christ and the Gospels,* "Basin."

4. *Contra Helvidium,* 10.

5. *Ibid.*

6. Maldonatus, *Commentarii in Quatuor Evangelistas.*

7. *Élevations sur les Mystères.*

8. Hastings, *op. cit.,* "Swaddling Clothes."

9. Vigouroux, *Dictionnaire de la Bible,* "Langes."

10. Smith and Cheetham, *Dictionary of Christian Antiquities,* "St. Mary."

11. *Oratio de Resurrectione,* I.

12. *Sermo 123.*
13. *The Everlasting Man* (New York: Dodd, Mead & Co., 1939).

CHAPTER 14

1. *Jewish Encyclopedia*, "Hanukkah."
2. Edersheim, *The Life and Times of Jesus the Messiah* (New York: Longmans, Green and Co., 1925), 2, xiv.
3. Fouard, *The Christ the Son of God* (New York: Longmans, Green and Co., 1919), 2, viii.
4. *Oratio in sancto Lumine.*
5. *The Jewish Antiquities*, 12, 7, 7.
6. *Jewish Encyclopedia*, "Hanukkah."
7. Talmud, *Sanhedrin.*
8. Thomson, *The Land and the Book*, xiv.
9. *Epistle 108.*
10. *Onomasticon*, 43.
11. Meistermann, *Guide to the Holy Land* (New York: P. J. Kenedy & Sons, 1924), iv.
12. *Ibid.*
13. *Op. cit.*, 15, 10, 4.
14. Talmud, *Shekalim.*
15. Edersheim, *Sketches of Jewish Social Life* (New York: Fleming H. Revell Co.), v.

Selected Bibliography

A Lapide, *Commentaria in Quatuor Evangelia.*
Augustine, St., *De Sancta Virginitate.*

Bossuet, *Élevations sur les Mystères.*

Catholic Encyclopedia.
Chesterton, G. K., *The Everlasting Man. The New Jerusalem.*

Dictionary of Christ and the Gospels.
Dictionary of Christian Antiquities.
Dictionnaire Pratique des Connaissances Religieuses.

Edersheim, *The Life and Times of Jesus the Messiah. The Temple, Its Ministry and Services. Sketches of Jewish Social Life.*
Encyclopaedia Biblica.
Eusebius, *The Church History. The Life of Constantine.*

Farrar, *The Life of Christ.*
Felton, *Storia dei Tempi del Nuovo Testamento.*
Fillion, *Vie de Notre-Seigneur Jésus Christ.*
Fouard, *The Christ the Son of God.*

Graetz, *History of the Jews.*
Gregory of Nyssa, St., *Oratio de Resurrectione. Oratio in sancto Lumine.*

Hastings, *Dictionary of the Bible.*

Jameson, *Legends of the Madonna.*
Jerome, St., *Epistolae. Contra Helvidium.*

Jewish Encyclopedia.

Jones, *The Herods of Judaea.*

Josephus, Flavius, *The Jewish Antiquities. The Jewish War. The Life of Josephus. Against Apion.*

Justin Martyr, St., *Dialogue With Trypho.*

Kissane, *The Book of Isaiah.*

Lagrange, *Évangile selon Saint Luc. The Gospel of Jesus Christ. Le Judaïsme.*

Lebreton, *The Life and Teaching of Jesus Christ.*

Maldonatus, *Commentarii in Quatuor Evangelistas.*

Meistermann, *Guide to the Holy Land.*

Morton, *In the Steps of the Master.*

Ollivier, *De Bethléem à Nazareth.*

Origen, *Contra Celsum.*

O'Shea, *Mary and Joseph.*

Papini, *Life of Christ.*

Prat, *Jesus Christ.*

Ricciotti, *The Life of Christ.*

Sanday, and Waterhouse, *Sacred Sites of the Gospels.*

Schürer, *A History of the Jewish People in the Time of Jesus Christ.*

Singer, *The Authorised Daily Prayer Book of the United Hebrew Congregations.*

Smith, G. A., *Jerusalem.*

Smith, *Dictionary of the Bible.*

Stanley, *History of the Jewish Church. Sinai and Palestine.*

Tacitus, *The Annals. The History.*

Talmud, *Berakoth. Pirke Aboth. Sanhedrin. Shabbath. Shekalim. Yoma.*

Thomson, *The Land and the Book.*

Tissot, *The Life of Our Lord Jesus Christ.*

Vigouroux, *Dictionnaire de la Bible.*